Precious In His Sight

A Fresh Look at the Nature of Man

Harold R. Eberle

Winepress Publishing, Yakima, Washington

Precious In His Sight

© 1998 by Harold R. Eberle
First Printing, July 1998, produced under the title:
   People Are Good
Second Edition, First Printing, June 2000

Winepress Publishing
P.O. Box 10653
Yakima, WA 98909-1653
(509) 248-5837
www.winepress.org
winepress@nwinfo.net

Library of Congress Control No. 00-132995
ISBN 1-882523-18-0
Cover and graphic art by Eugene M. Holmes
Cover Photo by Janette Scheider

Printed in the United States of America

Credits and Thanks

The second edition of this book, which you now hold in your hands, has the added input of over 30 ministers and church leaders. Not only have friends too numerous to mention helped in editing these pages, but the contents have been the topic of open discussion at three significant gatherings where ministers made comments and added their insights. Keith Gerner, a fellow minister, spoke words that brought clarification to the discussion in chapter 17. I also need to thank my students at Destiny Bible College for their input, especially Susan Silvernail. In addition, Pastor Pete Eisenman, Greg Correll, James Bryson and Pastor Steve Johnson left their marks on these pages.

Most important, I need to thank Pastor James Leuschen. Chapter 8, titled, "Born in Sin?" and chapter 18, titled "The Nature of Jesus" were developed almost completely from his own work on this subject. In addition, Pastor Leuschen's teachings have influenced my thinking profoundly. Although I take full responsibility—credit or fault—his comments, advice and challenges have caused me to study, think deeply and communicate more clearly.

Linda Eberle, my precious wife, and Edward Eberle, my father, helped me believe in people as described herein. Dennis Jacobson, Ron and Peggy Graham, and Annette Bradley helped with the editing process.

Let's change the world together!

Table of Contents

Introduction

I have been set free. As many of my Christian friends, I was enslaved to a negative view of mankind. I had no idea how strongly it gripped my life and influenced every decision I made. A new perspective from the Word of God has made my life freer, more hopeful and more effective in ministering the gospel.

Introduction

CHAPTER 1

Our Lord's Perspective

I used to suspect all people of being basically evil. That way of thinking seems to have been programmed into my mind from years of associating with other Christians who hold this view. I erroneously had concluded that everyone is basically evil until they receive Jesus into their life. I considered the salvation experience as the transition point between evilness and goodness. This simplistic way of thinking seemed reasonable at the time.

However, I discovered that our Lord Jesus did not generalize that all non-Christians were evil. As I read through the New Testament, I found that He repeatedly spoke, comparing good versus bad people, without reference to any Christian experience. This surprised me!

For example, in Matthew 5:45 we read our Lord's words:

"...He causes His sun to rise on the

> *evil and the good, and sends rain on*
> *the righteous and the unrighteous."*

This assumes that there are both good and evil people in the world. Yet, Jesus was not speaking in terms of Christians versus non-Christians. He was speaking of the whole of humanity—people who had not even heard the gospel yet.

When I realized that Jesus recognized both good and evil people on the earth, I had to conclude that my earlier way of thinking was wrong. Not all non-Christians are evil.

Now, as I point this out, I am not denying that every human sins. I will make this point over and over again throughout this book, lest some wrongly conclude that I am teaching that people do not need Jesus as their Savior. Of course, *that is not what I am saying.* Please hear these words correctly. All people sin and all people need forgiveness for their sins.

Furthermore, when I talk about *good people,* I am not saying that they are good in the sense of *perfection.* The adjective *good,* as used in the New Testament, most commonly is interpreted from the Greek word *agathos. Agathos* can mean *good* in the sense of *perfection,* or it can be used in a less strict, but still very positive way.

For example, when a certain man came to Jesus and called Him *"Good Teacher,"* Jesus answered:

*"Why do you call Me good? No one is
good except God alone."*
(Mark 10:18)

The goodness spoken of here has to do with
perfection—a standard which no human being
can attain.

We can see the word *good* (*agathos* in Greek)
being used in other passages in a less strict
sense, such as Luke 23:50, which describes
Joseph:

> *And behold, a man named Joseph,
> who was a member of the Council, a
> good and righteous man....*

The Bible is not contradicting itself when it
says in one verse that no one is good, and then in
other verses points out certain people who are,
indeed, good. Rather, the word *good* can be used
in different ways.

If we use the term *good* the way the Bible
uses the term, we can say that certain people are
good, realizing that this does not necessarily
mean perfection.

With this understanding, we can see how our
Lord Jesus referred to some people as good and
righteous, while He referred to other people as
evil and unrighteous. The amazing point for our
discussion is how our Lord used these descriptive
terms independently of any Christian experience. Yes, non-Christians can be good.

Consider our Lord's words in the following Bible passage:

> *"The good man out of his good treasure brings forth what is good...."*   (Matt. 12:35)

The good man to whom He refers did not receive his goodness as a result of a salvation experience. No, Jesus was talking about people who never had heard His saving message.

We can see biblical evidence of goodness within man in other passages also. For example, the description of a Gentile named Cornelius reads this way:

> *...a devout man, and one who feared God with all his household....*
> (Acts 10:2)

> *...a righteous and God-fearing man....*   (Acts 10:22)

At the time these words were spoken, Cornelius had not heard about Jesus. Yet, he is said to be righteous, devout and fearing God.

The term *righteous* also is used by our Lord when referring to certain people who lived during the Old Testament times. For example, when Jesus was rebuking the Pharisees, He blamed them and their forefathers for killing the righteous men and women who previously had been sent by God:

> *...that upon you may fall the guilt of all the righteous blood shed on the earth, from the blood of righteous Abel to the blood of Zechariah....*
>
> (Matt. 23:35)

This verse implies that there were *numerous* people in the Old Testament times who could be considered righteous.

The reason this is important to note is because many Christians think (as I formerly thought) we should use the descriptive term *righteous* only when referring to born-again Christians. What has been eye-opening to many of us is realizing how Jesus and the writers of the Bible used the term *righteous* to describe many non-Christians.

Of course, we should make a distinction in how we use this word. We realize that no one is perfect, and that compared with God and in His sight "no man living is righteous" (Ps. 143:2). In that sense, only Jesus Christ can be said to be perfectly righteous. However, the term *righteous* also can be used in a less strict sense. We can, as the Bible does, recognize that some people are righteous—not in comparison with God—but, indeed, they do have a quality of holiness and uprightness about their lives.

Many individuals in the Old Testament are said to be righteous and/or good; for example, Noah (Gen. 6:9), Josiah (II Chron. 34:2-3), Enoch (Gen. 5:22), Job (Job 1:1), and others whom we will discuss later. Jesus had not yet died for the

7

forgiveness of these people's sins. Men and women in the Old Testament times were not born again. Yet, many are referred to as being good, righteous, holy, blameless and fearing God.

This leaves us with an important question: What is man's condition in his natural state? Is man's nature basically evil? These are the questions which I will answer in the study to follow.

However, we cannot approach this subject fairly without an openness to truth. Many Christians have fixed so firmly in their minds the doctrine that says man in his basic nature is evil, that they cannot consider anything which contradicts their present beliefs—even if they are the words of our Lord Jesus Christ. The plain truth is that you cannot believe mankind is naturally evil and at the same time believe the words of Jesus.

> You cannot believe both the words of Jesus and the doctrine that says all non-Christian people are evil.

Before we proceed, allow me to repeat: I acknowledge that apart from Jesus no one is *good* or *righteous* in the sense of being *perfect*. All people sin. Everyone needs forgiveness. We all need a Savior who is Jesus Christ. Whether people are good or bad, they all fall short of the glory of God (Rom. 3:23).

Having stated that again, let's continue on a course to discover truth.

8

CHAPTER 2

Historical Influences

As I began to realize that my previously held negative view of mankind was not completely accurate, I determined to discover how I had arrived at my wrong way of thinking. Certainly, it was shared by a large percentage of the Christians with whom I had been associated. This implies that something in our past contributed to our shared beliefs. Sure enough, if we study Church history, we can find specific times when teachings on man's nature became very negative.

For example, during the Protestant Reformation of the 1500s, several leaders made very strong points concerning the evilness of man in his unregenerate state. Leaders, such as Martin Luther and John Calvin, especially are known for their stand on the inherent evilness of man. This became a basic tenet of their faith because, above all else, they wanted to emphasize the truth of salvation by grace through faith. In their efforts to emphasize this truth, they expounded on the evilness of man, and how that no one can get to heaven by "works." The more evil they portrayed man, the easier it was to show the need for Jesus' death. In fact, most of the leaders of the Reformation taught that man was *totally depraved*, which means man is totally and completely evil, unable to do anything good until after he is saved.

We can honor the men and women of God who so courageously put forth the message of salvation by grace through faith; however, we also can realize that their forceful stance led them to interpret certain Scriptures through distorted eyes. For example, one of the verses most commonly used to teach wrongly that man is totally depraved is Isaiah 64:6, which says:

> *For all of us have become like one*
> *who is unclean,*
> *And all our righteous deeds are like*
> *a filthy garment....*

The Reformers of the 1500s taught from this verse (and I formerly taught) that everything the natural man does—even that which seems righteous—is evil in God's eyes.

All we have to do is read the context of this verse to see how wrong this interpretation is. For example, the preceding verse (Is. 64:5) tells us how God responds readily and willingly to people who do righteous deeds:

> *Thou dost meet him who rejoices in*
> *doing righteousness....*(Is. 64:5)

Seeing this verse, we must conclude that verse six neither is condemning nor rejecting a human being's acts of righteousness. They are not always "filthy garments" in God's eyes.

The truth is that Isaiah 64:6 is speaking about the condition of the Jewish people during the time they were exiled to Babylon. The prophet Isaiah is crying out to God and recalling how God once looked with favor upon them as a people. Notice how verse six says that they all "have become" like one who is unclean. They were not always rejected by God, but came to a point in their rebellion against God where, indeed, He did turn His favor away from them.

To remove verse six from its context, and then apply it to all people in every generation, is a serious mistake. Furthermore, it is wrong to isolate the verse and apply it to ourselves, saying that all of *our* righteous deeds are as a filthy garment.

The Reformers interpreted other Bible verses through such a negative filter, as well. We will examine some of those verses as we continue, but here our goal is to identify how that negative thinking originated.

Today, Christians who believe in the "total depravity" of man rarely realize how much they have been influenced by the Reformed Theology of the 1500s. Again, we can accept much of what those leaders accomplished for Christianity;

however, it is time we examined the Scriptures more carefully to separate the truth from what the Reformers over-emphasized in their struggle to establish the doctrine of "salvation by grace, through faith."

Again, allow me to repeat that I believe salvation is given to us by grace. All people sin and all people need a Savior who is Jesus Christ. However, it is wrong to say that man in his natural state is totally depraved.

Another period in history during which the total-depravity view became embraced among Christians is after the fourth century, when the teachings of Augustine became predominant in the established Church. Augustine (354-430 A.D.) taught that all people inherit the sin and guilt of Adam. Furthermore, Augustine taught that the nature of man is so evil that man cannot even choose to move toward God.

Augustine defined and clarified his beliefs as he debated another theologian named Pelagius. Pelagius, a British monk, rejected the idea of original sin and taught that people are born innocent. In that time period, thousands of Christians aligned their views with each side of the argument. However, in 416 A.D., Augustine called a synod of bishops to settle this debate, and as a result, was able to convince Pope Innocent I to denounce Pelagius.*

---

* For the sake of readers who are familiar with the teachings of Pelagius, allow me to say that I will not be fully embracing Pelagian thought; I dare say that he went too far in his arguments on the inherent goodness of man.

Although Augustine "won" the battle with Pelagius, the Roman Catholic Church did not embrace completely Augustine's negative view of man. Pope Gregory, for example, softened Augustine's view by saying that man inherits sin but not Adam's guilt. Thomas Aquinas, who often is accepted by Roman Catholics as the greatest theologian in history, taught that man's will is *bent by sin*, although it is not determined to evil completely.

Among Eastern Orthodox Christians there are varying views, although the majority of teachers would say that all of mankind received death and corruption through Adam, but not the guilt of Adam.

Although there have been many other leaders in Church history who have taught varying views concerning the nature of man, we should note that those mentioned above are still very influential in our present-day concept of man's nature. Whether Protestant, Roman Catholic or Orthodox, all of us—to some degree—have been influenced by those who have gone before us.

As we continue, we will delve further into "Reformed Theology," that is, the doctrinal beliefs laid out by those leaders of the Reformation in the 1500s. It is important to understand that Reformed Theology is at the very foundation of what is called today "Evangelical Christianity." Today's Evangelical Christians have changed, modified and grown in several areas from what their Reformed forefathers believed and taught; however, they still hold to the same basic tenets.

Just as Evangelical Christians do, I believe that the Bible is the inspired, infallible Word of God. Therefore, I will be developing my views from the Holy Scriptures. However, I will challenge the doctrine concerning the inherent evilness of man, and then explain why we Bible-believing Christians cannot accept it.

In the pages to follow, I will present a fresh view on the nature of man, developing one principle upon another. For the reader who is eager to understand the implications of this teaching, he/she can jump ahead to the last four chapters of this book (chapters 25-28). There I have discussed how these truths can change your life. However, I hope each reader will take the time to follow through the discussion ahead.

Created in God's Image

Consider how God created the first man:

> *Then the LORD God formed man of dust from the ground, and breathed into his nostrils the breath of life; and man became a living being.*
>
> (Gen. 2:7)

This was a creative, wonderful act, beyond our full comprehension.

> *And God created man in His own image, in the image of God He created him; male and female He created them.* (Gen. 1:27)

After God finished creating all that He had made, He saw that it was "very good" (Gen. 1:31). Man was included in this description. In what way was he good? Was he good spiritually?

Intellectually? Emotionally? Morally? Yes. God's description of man as "very good" included his entire being. God did a good job in what He created.

Even though Adam and Eve were created good, they still were *vulnerable to sin.* The descriptive term, "good," did not include complete protection from all evil. No, Satan was able to tempt them.

After Adam and Eve submitted to Satan's temptation, did they and all future mankind lose the image of God in which they were created? No. God declared in Genesis 9:6 that no person is ever to kill another person, because all people are made in the image of God:

> *"Whoever sheds man's blood,*
> *By man his blood shall be shed,*
> *For in the image of God*
> *He made man."*

Further, we can read in the New Testament concerning man's nature:

> *...he is the image and glory of God....*
> (I Cor. 11:7)

Notice, man is still the image and glory of God—even after the fall of Adam and Eve.

When I talk about man being the image and glory of God, I am not equating man with God. A good analogy is that of a toy airplane being made in the image of a real airplane. In similar

16

fashion, man was made in the image and glory of God.

Another analogy I can make is how the ocean can spray a mist of water onto the shore. Similarly, God released a breath from His nature into Adam's being. Even though the breath which sustains man's life may become contaminated by sin, still at its most basic structure it bears the same characteristics of the substance from which it came.

Even the *glory* of man is an important and sustained element in his being. Of course, man's glory is not as great as God's glory. Romans 3:23 tells us that we all "fall short of the glory of God." However, man still has glory in his nature. In fact, all created things do. The apostle Paul compares the different aspects of creation, saying there is one flesh of birds and another of beasts; and there is one glory of the stars and another glory of the sun and moon (I Cor. 15:38-41). There is glory in every aspect of God's creation.

So then, we must realize that man—even after the fall—to some degree still exists in the image and glory of God.

Think about this: If we had been created in Satan's image, then we would be evil by creation. However, we have been created in God's image. Obviously, something happened when Adam and Eve sinned (which we will study in the chapters to follow); however, we must keep in mind that man is still created in the image and glory of God.

God Is Not Like That

Adam and Eve sinned. Does that mean every human being is born with the judgment, consequences, guilt, sin tendencies and/or curse of that sin?

Let's see what God says about this.

In Exodus 20:5-6, we read God's words as He spoke from Mount Sinai, revealing who He is:

> *"...for I, the LORD your God, am a jealous God, visiting the iniquity of the fathers on the children, on the third and the fourth generations of those who hate Me, but showing lovingkindness to thousands, to those who love Me and keep My commandments."*

Notice that God said the sins of the parents will be visited upon the children to the third and fourth generations. This implies that the sins of parents may influence children, grandchildren and great-grandchildren. This is a sobering truth which often is taught in Christian churches today. Of course, we believe it.

However, notice the primary message of this Bible passage. It is not just about sin and judgment. It is about God. This is God's declaration from Mount Sinai concerning who He is. And what do we learn about God? He is jealous. Furthermore, He is the kind of God who allows the sins of the parents to go to the third or fourth generation. More significantly, however, is the fact that He gives His lovingkindness to thousands of generations. The main point in these verses is that *His love goes much further* than man's sin. This is the kind of God we have.

These verses reassure us that sin will **not** be passed on to ten, twenty, thirty or more generations. Only His love would go that far. God is **not** the kind of God who would let the sin of Adam and Eve come upon people who are hundreds or thousands of generations later.

To accuse God of being the kind of God who would make us, who are many generations later, suffer for the sins of Adam, is to reject the God who spoke from Mount Sinai and to reject what God declared about Himself in Exodus 20:5-6.

Furthermore, we must note that God said He would visit the sins of parents only upon "those who hate Me." God does not put judgment, curses or sin itself upon children *unless they hate God.* This means that sin is not passed automatically from parent to child. God said that He would allow the sins of parents to be visited upon the children *only if* during their lifetime they become antagonistic toward Him. It is not an *automatic* transference of evil, but something that comes upon them only if they, themselves, open their hearts to evil.*

Now let's add to this teaching. We already saw that God will not allow the sins of parents to be passed on automatically. But how about the punishment for those sins? Will the punishment or consequences of parents' sins be passed on to their children?

God spoke through the prophet Ezekiel:

> *The person who sins will die. The son will not bear the punishment for the father's iniquity, nor will the father bear the punishment for the son's iniquity; the righteousness of the righteous will be upon himself, and the wickedness of the wicked will be upon himself.*
>
> (Ezek. 18:20)

God said it: "The son will not bear the punishment for the father's iniquity."

In spite of this clear teaching, many Christians today believe that Adam's sin and the

---

* In chapter 17, more will be discussed about the sins of parents influencing later generations or what is sometime called "generational sins."

punishment for his sin have been passed on to every human being. In fact, some Christians have been indoctrinated so firmly into this way of thinking that they hold to the "inherited evilness of man" as a basic tenet of their faith.

In the next chapter and in chapter ten, we will examine what Adam's sin actually released, but please keep in mind what God has declared about Himself. He is not the kind of God who would let the sins of parents or the punishment for those sins come upon the generations to follow. To say that Adam's sin has been passed on to all of mankind is to accuse God of doing something which He clearly said He would not do.

CHAPTER 5

Sin Came Into the World

Some Christians (those adhering to Reformed Theology) incorrectly believe that all people inherit the judgment, consequences, guilt, sin tendencies and/or curse of the sin that Adam committed. The Bible verse most often used to promote this false doctrine is Romans 5:12:

> *Therefore, just as through one man sin entered into the world, and death through sin, and so death spread to all men, because all sinned....*

From this verse, it often has been taught that through Adam's sin, every descendant of Adam— that is, every human being—inherits sin, guilt and/or an evil nature.

Look carefully at this verse and see what it actually says. Is sin passed on to every person because of Adam's sin? I emphatically say, "No!"

What this verse (and other Bible verses I will discuss) tells us is that sin *"entered into the world"* because of Adam's sin. In the original Greek language in which our New Testament was written, we are told that sin entered into the *cosmos*, that is, the *world*. The Bible does *not* say that sin entered into the inherited nature of mankind.

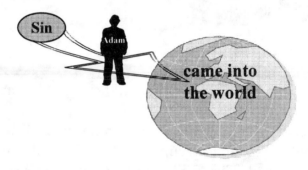

If we go back to study Church history, we easily can find out where people got the wrong interpretation of Romans 5:12. Augustine (354-430 A.D.) is most known for his teaching that sin entered into every human being because of Adam's sin. When we go back to follow his reasoning, we find that he was using a Latin translation of the New Testament, rather than the original manuscripts which were written and transcribed in Greek. Even though Augustine was a very influential Christian leader, he never learned to read Greek. In his Latin translation of Romans 5:12, the last phrase says *in quo omnes peccaverunt*. This means "in whom all have sinned." If Augustine's translation had been accurate, then, indeed, it could mean that *all people sin in Adam.* However, his Latin translation was incorrect.

What Romans 5:12 actually tells us in the original Greek language is "because all sinned." Therefore, we did <u>not</u> all sin in Adam. Romans 5:12 tells us that sin entered the *cosmos,* and not the *inherited nature* of man.

First John 2:16 tells us where sin abides:

> *For all that is in the world, the lust of the flesh and the lust of the eyes and the boastful pride of life, is not from the Father, but is from the world.*

Sin abides in the world, that is, the *cosmos.*

Of course, we know that all people yield to the sin which is in the world. Therefore, the sin which is in the cosmos becomes active in their lives, too. As we associate with people, the sin which influences them acts upon each of us. Sin, therefore, works through their lives—that is, through the lives of our parents, friends, teachers, leaders, entertainers, movie makers, etc. We are vulnerable to the sin which is active in the world and in the people around us. Yes, sin is a powerful force. Every human being submits at some time during his or her life.

The main point is this: *Man is not born sinful; however, he is vulnerable, and, therefore, becomes sinful.*

At this point I should clarify what is meant by the terminology, "the fall of man." Although this phrase does not appear anywhere in the Bible, it has become commonly used in many Christian circles. When teachers holding to Reformed Theology say "the fall of man," they are implying that when Adam sinned, every human being became sinful. They err in the same way that Augustine did in mistranslating Romans 5:12.

I am teaching something very different in this book. Again, I should stress that the terminology, "the fall of man," is nowhere in the Bible. However, if a Christian chooses to use this terminology, I could agree only that man has fallen in the sense that he has fallen *out of the fullness of God's grace, under the power of Satan,* and *under the power of death* (which will be discussed more in a later chapter). However, man has *not* fallen in the sense of his nature becoming inherently evil. That is not what the Bible teaches.

Please make this distinction in your mind: sin came into the world, not into the inherited nature of man. Let's study further to establish this truth.

CHAPTER 6

Romans One and Two

Christians very often use the book of Romans to develop fundamental doctrines pertaining to the nature of man, sin and salvation. This is because the apostle Paul lays out clear doctrinal views, building one upon another in this book. In chapters one and two, Paul discusses the basic nature of man. Let's examine his description to see what he teaches.

After Paul gives an introduction and greeting to the Roman Christians, he explains that every human being is created with a knowledge or an awareness of God:

> *...because that which is known about God is evident within them; for God made it evident to them.*
>
> (Rom. 1:19)

The nature of God is revealed in all creation and within every human being. There is something deposited in each human being from birth that declares who God is.

The reason Paul began the book of Romans in this way is because he wanted to show that no person has an excuse. Whether or not they ever hear the gospel message during their lifetime, all of creation declares that there is a God. There is also within every human being a conscience—an awareness, an inner-knowing that God is real.

Now, some people may object to this truth, saying that there are atheists who do not believe in God. I must respond by saying, "Nonsense!" Some people *claim* to be atheists, but in light of Paul's words, we must conclude that all people have resident within their innermost beings an awareness of God's existence. They may try to deny it. They may try to cover this fact with years of brainwashing themselves. They may develop, as the Bible says, a seared conscience (I Tim. 4:2), which calluses over the truth; but in reality, every human being is created by God with an awareness that there is a God.

As King Solomon wrote, God has set eternity in the heart of man (Eccl. 3:11).

For natural evidence of this fact, all we have to do is study people groups all over the world, either present today or in history. People always have sought to worship a divine being. They may develop misinformation concerning who He is, but the awareness of God is in the nature of man.

Of course, there are many people who do not worship any God, and some who even deny His existence. But what I hope you see is that they all are living in denial of a witness that God has planted within their very being.

Paul explained in Romans 1:21-32, that as people give themselves over to sin, their minds become depraved and their hearts darkened:

> For even though *they knew God,* they did not honor Him as God, or give thanks; but they became futile in their speculations, and their foolish heart was darkened.
> (Rom. 1:21, emphasis added)

Notice that at the start, all people "knew God," but darkness, denial and atheism is a clouding of the mind that later comes upon people who give themselves over to sin.

Paul repeated this, saying:

> Therefore God gave them over in the lusts of their hearts to impurity.... For they *exchanged the truth of God* for a lie....
> (Rom. 1:24-25, emphasis added)

As people yield to sin, they become corrupt, but they start out with a knowledge of the "truth of God."

We can go one step further in our investigation of man's nature by reading chapter two of Romans and discovering Paul's main point. He explains that no human being has an excuse for sin, because people are created not only with an awareness of God's existence, but also with a consciousness of right and wrong:

> *For when Gentiles who do not have the Law do instinctively the things of the Law, these, not having the Law, are a law to themselves, in that they show the work of the Law written in their hearts, their conscience bearing witness, and their thoughts alternately accusing or else defending them....*
>
> (Rom. 2:14-15)

Paul is speaking here of Gentiles who never were exposed to the Law as given by God in the Old Testament. He said even they—*instinctively* or *by nature*—do the things of the Law.

Just as wild animals have instincts that, to some degree, direct their behavior, so also do people. A baby looks to its mother from the moment of birth (and even before). A mother desires to care for her child. A father has an instinctive code written within to protect and provide for his family.

Of course, there are people who deny these instinctive behaviors, and subsequently kill or abandon their children. There are fathers who do not care for their families. However, people know better. They consciously must disregard the natural (instinctive) tendencies when they commit such sins.

The instinctive behaviors go beyond basic survival skills. The apostle Paul wrote about the Gentiles *doing the Law of God instinctively.* These things are written on the hearts of people. Every human knows that adultery and murder are wrong. They may deny it. They may give themselves over to related sins to such a degree that their minds cloud the facts. But the natural awareness of right and wrong is instinctive, that is, implanted within us by God.

It is important that we identify this awareness of right and wrong as "more than a conscience." When the term *conscience* is used today, it often is limited to a *mental* awareness of right and wrong. Paul includes a mental recognition in his explanation, but he also tells us that the Gentiles, and by implication, every human being, has the law written on his or her "heart."

Yes, there is a pre-assigned, already-written code on the heart of every human being. It comes by nature.

Think about this: "What is natural for a person to do, and what is unnatural?" As I mentioned, it is natural or instinctive for a newborn baby to need its mother; this is natural, beautiful and right. It is natural for a mother to care for her children. It is natural and right for a father to endeavor to provide for his family. These are according to God's will, and a person is born with these instinctive tendencies.

Of course, there are people who violate these instinctive behaviors; however, I hope you see such violations as "unnatural." It is unnatural for a parent to abandon his or her children. Hurting and/or murdering other people is unnatural. It is these unnatural acts that are against God's will.

Concerning the unnatural, Paul gave examples to the Romans (chapters one and two) about people who give themselves over to sexual sins:

> ...*women exchanged the <u>natural</u> <u>function</u> for that which is un- natural, and in the same way also the men abandoned the <u>natural</u> <u>function</u> of the woman and burned in their desire toward one another, men with men committing indecent acts....*
> (Rom. 1:26-27, emphasis added)

In this passage, Paul was referring to homo- sexuality and other sexual perversions. He labeled these as unnatural, indecent and evil. On the other hand, the natural desires are good.

When people give themselves over to unnatural desires, they sin. When they yield to natural desires, they live according to God's will.

Many Christians have reversed this in their minds. They think sin is natural, but it is not according to Paul's words here. Of course, everyone sins, and I will discuss this as we continue. But here, I hope you realize that the natural tendencies within man are according to God's will.

If we are going to accept the apostle Paul's understanding of the nature of man, as taught in Romans one and two, we must see that people begin in life with:

1. a witness of God
2. knowledge of the truth of God
3. natural desires to do God's will

At this point many of my readers may be having questions arise within their minds concerning the *sinful nature of man*. Those influenced by Reformed teaching have been trained to think that man is *born sinful*. As we continue, I will show that man is *not born* with a sinful nature; however, he *develops* a sinful nature as he yields to the evil which is in the world (*cosmos*). Man starts off in life as Paul describes in the preceding discussion. However, he *becomes sinful* and *takes on a sinful nature*.

Before we go on, consider another passage from the Bible which refers to the good qualities in the natural man. Consider what our Lord Jesus stated, as recorded in Matthew 5:46:

> *For if you love those who love you, what reward have you? Do not even the tax-gatherers do the same?*

33

In the context of this passage, Jesus was exhorting us to go beyond the natural person's ability and love all people. Of course, we hear His words and desire to have divine love which encompasses all people. However, we should not miss the underlying truth that even the natural man—the sinner—loves his family and others close to him.

Some Christians are so completely negative about the nature of man, they won't even admit that non-Christians are capable of love. They like to quote I John 4:19, which says, "We love, because He first loved us." Those with a strictly Reformed view will use this verse to imply that only Christians can love, because only they have experienced God's love.

In reality, I John is talking about how God's love will expand in us and cause us to encompass our brothers and sisters in Christ. Indeed, we see that truth; however, to say that non-Christians are incapable of love is not true.

As a matter of fact, Jesus recognized that even the natural man has love for his own family and for those who love him in return. That kind of love is natural. *That is how God created us.*

CHAPTER 7

Babies Are Innocent

I am teaching that man is created in God's image and that there is something good in man. Now let's take a closer look at babies. What is their condition when they come into the world?

Consider our Lord's view of children. He testified to the innocence of children, saying:

> *"Truly I say to you, unless you are converted and become like children, you shall not enter the kingdom of heaven."* (Matt. 18:3)

> *"Yes; have you never read, 'Out of the mouth of infants and nursing babes Thou hast prepared praise for Thyself'?"* (Matt. 21:16b)

> *"Let the children alone, and do not hinder them from coming to Me; for the kingdom of heaven belongs to such as these."* (Matt. 19:14b)

Our Lord made these statements in the context of contrasting the condition of infants with the condition of adults. We must conclude that there is some degree of innocence and holiness associated with children.

Furthermore, we can see that children have some "divine connection" with God. Matthew records our Lord's words when He said:

> *"See that you do not despise one of these little ones, for I say to you, that their angels in heaven continually behold the face of My Father who is in heaven."* (Matt. 18:10)

Notice that the angels assigned to children have direct access to God. Because of this, we are told not to despise any infant. In other words, our attitude toward children should be influenced by an awareness of how their angels stand openly before God. *Yes, there is a very real association between infants and God's presence.*

Christians under Reformed Theology teach that everyone comes into this world *alienated* from God. They teach that because of Adam's sin all of us come into this world with a sinful nature, and, therefore, separated from God. That view is contrary to the perspective of children which our Lord gives us.

As I address this subject of children, I need to speak not only from a theological point of view, but also from a practical, experiential position.

Parents—including my wife and me—have raised children, and hence, know firsthand that there is a certain innocence within infants, yet also a more negative—even selfish—side to their nature.

How do we understand this? Are children evil from birth? Did they inherit sinfulness?

In chapter three I explained how God does not pass on the sin of Adam to thousands of generations of his descendants. At the same time we recognized that sins of parents can influence children to the third or fourth generation. In chapter 17, I will write more about those three-to-four-generation sin influences, but here I want to address the *basic negative tendencies* which are evident and common in all children.

For example, it would be common for two young siblings to argue over a certain toy. Children do not have to be taught how to quarrel in such situations. They seem to have these instinctive behaviors from birth.

Is this sin?

Christians with a Reformed theological view would say "yes," and in order to emphasize this, they immediately would point out other similar behaviors which seem to indicate an inherited evil nature.

However, that would be only a superficial conclusion. I can challenge it by showing that animals have similar behaviors. For example, two wild fox pups will fight over a piece of meat or even a stick. We would not accuse these fox pups of being sinners, and we never would conclude that the fox pups inherited an evil nature from Adam. No, that is not a reasonable explanation.

The truth is that God instilled certain survival tendencies within the fox pups that are necessary for their continued existence. In the same way, there are instinctive behaviors within humans that we cannot condemn as sin. Yes, they may appear selfish from an outsider's perspective. However, we cannot label them as sinful, otherwise we must accuse animals of being sinful, as well. That would be foolish.

This is no small issue. Christians who believe in total depravity build much of their case on the fact that children will act independently and do not need to be taught how to rebel against their parents. The Christian steeped in Reformed thinking will repeat the age-old question, "Why will a toddler stamp his foot and say, 'No,' to his or her parents?" Those with a Reformed view will expect us to conclude that this is proof that a child is born with a sin nature.

Such thinking is wrong. This is a perfect example of how an engineered question can steer the discussion down a distorted path. We just as easily could ask the positive question, "Why do children do many good things, such as express love to their parents, tenderly care for their younger siblings, or obey their parents?" This question is just as valid as the Reformers' question. *Furthermore, it is wrong to ask the negatively focused question without asking the positively oriented one.* If negative behavior implies that a child has a sinful nature, then by the same reasoning positive behavior implies that the child is born with a good nature. Anyone who raises children knows that both behaviors are possible and frequent.

What is wrong with the Reformers' logic? It comes down to their understanding of sin and evil. As we continue, we will develop a better understanding of what sin is. Here I can point out that "...sin is not imputed when there is no law" (Rom. 5:13). This means that God does not label negative behavior as sin, unless there is law; that is, unless there is an awareness of right and wrong. The apostle Paul also stated this truth in Romans 4:15, explaining, "...but where there is no law, neither is there violation."

Yes, there is an "age of accountability." As children grow they become more and more aware of right and wrong. As I mentioned earlier, there is a God-instilled sense of right and wrong in every human being, but there is also a progressive awareness of it.

There is a clear biblical correlation between the knowledge of right and wrong and an awareness of one's own nakedness. We can see this by reading the Genesis account of Adam and Eve. Before they sinned, they were innocent, naked and unashamed (Gen. 2:25). Immediately after they ate of the tree of the knowledge of good and evil, we are told:

> *Then the eyes of both of them were
> opened, and they knew that they
> were naked; and they sewed fig
> leaves together and made themselves
> loin coverings.* (Gen. 3:7)

Please take note of this relationship between sin and an awareness of one's nakedness.

Neither animals nor infants are aware of their own nakedness. This is evidence of the fact that they as yet have not had their eyes opened to know right from wrong.

In summary, I am saying that infants are innocent, unaware of right and wrong. Of course, they may engage in some activities which appear selfish. However, self-preservational behaviors, and even independent thinking, cannot be included in our definition of sin prior to consciousness of right and wrong. Otherwise, all animals would have to be judged as sinful, and that is an unbiblical judgment. Furthermore, God is not the kind of God who condemns children of sin before they are aware of right and wrong.

Jesus saw children as innocent, and we must also. He instructed us not to despise nor look negatively upon them, because their angels continually behold the face of the Father. Children do not come into this world alienated from God. In fact, there is some unique and precious association between them and the presence of God.

CHAPTER 8

Born in Sin?

There is a specific Scripture verse from the Old Testament which is often misused to teach that people are born evil. It is so frequently misused that it is worth mentioning at this point.

In Psalm 51:5, King David cries out to God in repentance, saying:

> *Behold, I was brought forth in iniquity,*
> *And in sin my mother conceived me.*

Some Christians have taught from this verse that every human being is born in sin and with a sinful nature.

Is that what King David was saying?

First of all, I must point out that there is no basis for taking what David says about his *own* conception and applying it to *every* human being. It is wrong, therefore, to use this passage as a description of every person's nature.

41

Next, we need to ask why David made this statement, even about himself. Did he mean that he himself was evil from the beginning?

That cannot be true because in other Psalms David wrote about his own relationship to God, even from birth. For example, in Psalm 22:9-10, he wrote:

> Yet Thou art He who didst bring me
>   forth from the womb;
> Thou didst make me trust when
>   upon my mother's breasts.
> Upon Thee I was cast from birth;
> Thou hast been my God from my
>   mother's womb.

In passages like these (see also Psalm 71:5-6), David contradicts the idea that he was evil from birth.

How can we explain this apparent contradiction? There are several plausible explanations for why David would say, "...in sin my mother conceived me."

First, we know that David's father was Jesse; however, the Bible reveals nothing about David's mother—neither name, nor origin. This is very unusual, because family lineages—especially of the kingly line—were of key importance in Hebrew thinking at that time. Because of this omission, later rabbis believed that David was born in adultery.* In light of this, think of

---

*Ellicott's Commentary on the Whole Bible, Vol. IV, page 61, © 1981, Zondervan: Grand Rapids, Michigan.

David's words: "...in sin my mother conceived me." Although we have no proof that David was conceived in adultery, it is a likely explanation.

This explanation is supported by the fact that David was given the role of shepherd boy in his own family. This was considered the lowest and most rejected family position. As a boy assigned to care for the sheep, it was very unlikely that he would ever have a chance to receive an education or be raised to a position of stature.

Furthermore, when the prophet Samuel came to anoint one of the sons of Jesse to be the next king, Jesse did not even present David along with his other sons (I Sam. 16:1-13). Only by God's intervention was David promoted within his family and eventually led the entire nation.

Another explanation of David's cry, "in sin my mother conceived me...," comes from a closer look at how David was expressing deep repentance throughout Psalm 51. This was David's prayer after he had been confronted by the prophet Nathan concerning his sins involving adultery with Bathsheba and the murder of Bathsheba's husband, Uriah. David was in repentance before the Lord, miserable and tormented. His mind was not making sober doctrinal statements, but his heart was gushing out the bitter cry of a man crushed by guilt. We must recognize that David was in this frame of mind and heart when he cried out these words.

Furthermore, in the presence of a holy God, men's sins can be magnified to the point to which they seem unbearable. For example, when Isaiah saw the Lord, he cried out:

> "...Woe is me, for I am ruined!
> Because I am a man of unclean lips,
> And I live among a people of unclean lips;
> For my eyes have seen the King,
> the LORD of hosts."   (Is. 6:5)

Notice how, in the glorious presence of God, Isaiah felt compelled to repent not only for his own sins but also for the sins of others. Even the fact that Isaiah lived among sinful people disqualified him and tainted him too much to behold God's holiness.

It is within the framework of that cognizance of God's holiness and David's own sins that we must interpret Psalm 51. We cannot take David's words as a doctrinal pronouncement. King David was overcome by his own sinfulness in the midst of God's holiness.

Using these perspectives, we would have to say that Psalm 51 is not teaching us that David was sinful from birth. If people approach this verse with the preconceived doctrine that man is sinful, they certainly could read into David's words that he was born a sinner. However, if they read David's words from the actual position in which he found himself, they should come to an entirely different conclusion. David was not saying he was born a sinner.

Refocus on David's words in Psalm 22:9-10:

> *Yet Thou art He who didst bring me*
> *forth from the womb;*
> *Thou didst make me trust when*
> *upon my mother's breasts.*
> *Upon Thee I was cast from birth;*
> *Thou hast been my God from my*
> *mother's womb.*

These verses describe a holy and pure beginning to David's life—even a relationship with God from birth.

Those Christians who are convinced that mankind is born in sin may try to discount Psalm 22:9-10 by saying that David really was speaking prophetically of Jesus Christ. Of course, we know that Jesus was born spotless and untouched by sin. Indeed, these verses may be applied to our Lord's condition at birth. However, this Psalm cannot be dismissed completely as having no meaning for David's own life. He sang this Psalm and taught the singers of his day to declare its message. In these words there has to be some personal significance for his own life, as well.

Those trained under Reformed Theology would rather disregard such words of David and fixate on the phrase, "...in sin my mother conceived me." I have shown how this phrase is better understood in light of his conception during an act of adultery and/or his cry of repentance before God. Furthermore, I pointed out that it is wrong to take David's words and apply them to all people of every generation. We were *not* all conceived in sin.

For final proof of this, we can read what the Bible tells us of John the Baptist, who was "...filled with the Holy Spirit, while yet in his mother's womb" (Luke 1:15). We cannot apply Psalm 51:5 to John the Baptist; therefore, it is wrong to apply it to every human being who ever has lived.

No, the Bible does not say that you and I were born in sin.

CHAPTER 9

Born with Original Sin?

We now need to ask if babies are born with "original sin."

As I define *original sin* and talk about the related doctrine, we will see that it is not taught in the Bible. In fact, Christians who have thought through the implications of original sin and the gospel come to the conclusion that they cannot believe both.

Allow me to show you.

Those who believe in *original sin* teach that every infant comes into this world already marked with sin. They believe that every baby is born with the stain of the sin which Adam and Eve committed in the Garden of Eden. That sin has been inherited, that is, passed on through the generational lines into the very nature of mankind. That inherited sin is called *original sin.*

Is it true that every baby is born with original sin?

Let's begin examining this by first obtaining a historical perspective of this doctrine. As I discussed in chapter five, the Bible verse most often used to teach that man is born in sin is Romans 5:12. Unfortunately, a mistranslation of this verse (the Latin Vulgate translation) says that in Adam all people have sinned.

Our earliest written records concerning the idea of original sin come from Cyprian, a Christian leader who lived in the third century. He taught that the stain of original sin could be removed only in baptism. *Before his time we have no historical evidence stating or implying that any Christians believed in original sin.*

It was Augustine (354-430 A.D.) who later popularized the doctrine. When we study his understanding of original sin, we find that he closely associated it with "sexual passion," which he considered evil. Augustine had a very negative view of sexual relations, even in marriage. He taught that every human being is conceived in sin because each of us are the result of a sexual union between our parents.

Looking back at Augustine's reasoning, we easily can see errors in his thinking. First is the fact that sexual relationships in marriage are not evil. Sex and sexual desires are a wonderful gift from God.

Second, we can challenge Augustine's thinking by pointing out that sexual passion could not be the avenue by which original sin is passed generation to generation. To see this, consider how our modern medical practices have enabled doctors to unite an egg and sperm outside the human body, in a sterile laboratory. Does this mean that such conceptions result in babies born without original sin? Obviously, Augustine never considered the implications of modern-day technology.

Today we easily can see the errors of Augustine's teaching; however, it is important to note that the doctrine of original sin, which he promoted, still permeates Christianity.

Let's look deeper.

Can sin be passed through the generational lines or genetic DNA? Consider the implications of the doctrine of original sin on the gospel itself.

If we believe the gospel, then we understand that when we put our faith in Jesus Christ, we become born again; our sins are forgiven and those sins have been separated from us "as far as the east is from the west" (Ps. 103:12). If we sin after becoming Christians, we can ask God to forgive us and He will. In fact, I John 1:9 reassures us:

> *If we confess our sins, He is faithful and righteous to forgive us our sins and to cleanse us from all unrighteousness.*

A foundational truth of the gospel is that we can be cleansed of sin.

Consider, then, what would happen if two Christians, who have been cleansed of all sin, had a child. Would that child be born with original sin? Well, the child could not have inherited the original sin, because the Bible tells us that the parents were cleansed of all sin. They could not pass on something which they did not possess. Therefore, the offspring of forgiven and cleansed Christian parents would have to be born without original sin.

Please do not misunderstand what I am saying here. I am not teaching that some people are born with original sin and others without it. No, that is not what I am saying. Rather I am showing you how illogical it is for Christians to say that they believe the gospel and at the same time that they believe everyone is born with original sin. The two beliefs are inconsistent and, in fact, contradict one another.

Personally, I do not believe anyone is born with original sin. Nowhere is it mentioned in the Bible. We have no historical evidence stating or implying that the first two centuries of Christians believed in it. The doctrine originated from a mistranslation of Romans 5:12. And most important, it is inconsistent with a fundamental truth of the gospel—you cannot believe both.

> You cannot be consistent and believe both the gospel and the doctrine of original sin.

CHAPTER 10

Consequences Of Adam's Sin

After Adam sinned, God spoke to Adam and told him what the consequences of his sin would be:

> *Cursed is the ground because of you;*
> *In toil you shall eat of it*
> *All the days of your life.*
> *Both thorns and thistles it shall*
>   *grow for you;*
> *And you shall eat the plants of the*
>   *field;*
> *By the sweat of your face*
> *You shall eat bread,*
> *Till you return to the ground,*
> *Because from it you were taken;*
> *For you are dust,*
> *And to dust you shall return."*
>   (Gen. 3:17b-19)

These consequences (along with several God spoke to Eve) have to do with the difficulties mankind will face while he is on this earth, plus the final sentence of death, at which time he will return to dust.

Certainly these consequences are serious and devastating. I do not want to minimize what happened as a result of Adam's sin. However, many Christians teach that *much more* happened than what God declared. In fact, Christians who agree with Reformed Theology teach that as a consequence of Adam's sin, every descendant of Adam (that is every human being) is stained with the sin of Adam, held guilty for Adam's sin and will spend eternity in hell unless redeemed.

According to Reformed Theology, these consequences are inherited. Newborn infants and adults possess them equally. The only escape from them is through receiving Jesus Christ as one's personal Savior.

Of course, I acknowledge that Jesus Christ is the only answer for man's problem of sin. I will repeat that truth over and over again throughout this book. What I am challenging here has to do with the consequences of Adam's sin. What did we actually inherit from Adam? What does the Bible tell us?

As God listed the consequences of Adam's sin, He did *not* mention either the stain of sin, the guilt of sin, or eternal damnation to hell for all of mankind. Doesn't that strike you as a major oversight on God's part? If it is true that billions of people will be sent to hell as a result of Adam's sin, don't you think that God would have mentioned it? Instead, God told Adam that he would work by the sweat of his brow and eventually return to dust. Compared to hell, these are extremely insignificant. In fact, we would have to admit that God's description was the greatest understatement in both the Bible and in recorded history.

Why didn't God declare the most devastating consequence which Reformed teachers believe is the result of Adam's sin? Because Reformed teachers are wrong in this instance. God knew what the consequences were and He stated them.

Consider more carefully what is meant by *death*. In certain contexts this word can mean more than physical death, and in some cases, it may even include *spiritual death*. In the next chapter I will discuss what is meant by *spiritual death*. Here I simply want to note that God was at least including physical death as He described the consequences of Adam's sin. In fact, God told Adam:

> *"...For you are dust,*
> *And to dust you shall return."*
> (Gen. 3:19)

There is no confusion about this. In this passage God was speaking about physical death as a result of the sin of Adam and Eve.

I can go one step further and say that physical death was a consequence of Adam's sin and was passed on to all of humanity. Every human being will die. Mankind lost immortality because of Adam's sin.

In the New Testament, the apostle Paul explained this truth to the Corinthian believers saying:

> *For since by a man came death, by a man also came the resurrection of the dead. For as in Adam all die, so also in Christ all shall be made alive.* (I Cor. 15:21-22)

In the context of this passage, Paul is talking about the hope of our future resurrection, that is, the resurrection of our physical bodies. Since Paul is comparing the resurrection of our bodies to the death which came through Adam, we know that he is speaking in this context of the physical death which resulted from Adam's sin. Yes, physical death came to all men through Adam, but resurrection life comes through Jesus Christ.

We also can look again at Romans 5:12 and see how death comes through sin:

> *Therefore, just as through one man sin entered into the world, and death through sin, and so death spread to all men, because all sinned—*

What are the results of Adam's sin? Sin came into the world and death through sin.

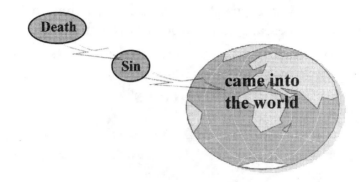

Paul goes on in Romans, chapter five, to tell us that this death *reigns* over all mankind. First, he states that death reigned over those people who lived before the law was given through Moses:

> *Nevertheless death reigned from Adam until Moses, even over those who had not sinned in the likeness of the offense of Adam....*   (Rom. 5:14)

Notice that death reigned over every human being from Adam to Moses even if they never had committed a sin like Adam's sin.

Next, Paul went on to explain how death reigns over all of mankind because of Adam's sin:

> *...by the transgression of the one, death reigned through the one....*
> (Rom. 5:17)

Like a king rules over people, so also death rules

over every person. Death, which is in the world because of Adam, has authority over mankind.

It is in this context that we can talk about the "fall of man." Indeed, mankind fell under the power of death. No one can escape its power: "...it is appointed for men to die once..." (Heb. 9:27). Every human being will die physically.

Having established this truth, let's go on to discuss *spiritual death*.

CHAPTER 11

Spiritual Death

Since Reformed Theology teaches that much more than physical death and difficulties in life resulted from Adam's sin, we need to examine its claims. The most important issue I need to discuss has to do with *spiritual death*. Teachers who follow Reformed Theology believe that Adam and Eve not only lost immortality, but actually died spiritually the day they sinned in the Garden of Eden. By this they mean that Adam's and Eve's spirits were separated from the life-giving God, and, therefore, lost vitality and became corrupted. Furthermore, Reformed teachers believe that the spiritual death of Adam and Eve is passed on inherently to every human being. In other words, every human being comes into this world with a dead spirit.

It is true that Adam and Eve experienced more than just physical death. I will agree with Reformed teachers concerning this. Before Adam and Eve ate of the forbidden fruit, God told them:

"...in the day that you eat from it you shall surely die." (Gen. 2:17)

Adam and Eve did experience some form of spiritual separation from God the day they disobeyed Him. In that sense, they did, indeed, die spiritually.

However, I disagree that spiritual death is passed on inherently to all the generations to follow. Yes, Adam died spiritually the day he ate of the forbidden fruit, but no, that condition of being separated from God was not and is not passed on to every human being. Let's review a few reasons which I already have discussed, and then add to our list.

1. As I noted in chapter four, God explicitly spoke from Mount Sinai and said that He would visit the sins of parents upon their children up to three or four generations, but only if they hated Him. In contrast, His lovingkindness would reach to thousands of generations. This is God's declaration concerning who He is. To say that spiritual death is inherently passed on to every generation is to deny the very nature of God and accuse Him of doing something which He said He would not do.

2. The apostle Paul explained in Romans 5:12 that sin came into the world (*cosmos*) because of Adam's sin. As I pointed out in chapter five, it was from a mistranslation of this verse that

leaders like Augustine developed the idea that sin came into the inherited nature of man.

3. In Romans, chapters one and two, Paul explained that people come into this world with a witness of God, knowledge of the truth of God and natural desires to do His will. People do not come into this world "anti-God," as Reformed teachers would have us think.

4. According to our Lord Jesus Christ, children are innocent. They do not come into this world alienated from God. In fact, as Jesus stated, their angels continually behold the face of the Father. There is some unique and precious association between them and the presence of God.

5. As I discussed in chapter eight, we have biblical examples of individuals who were descendants of Adam, and yet they were definitely not separated from God from birth. For example, John the Baptist was "...filled with the Holy Spirit, while yet in his mother's womb" (Luke 1:15). King David wrote:

> *Upon Thee I was cast from birth;*
> *Thou hast been my God from my*
> *mother's womb.* (Ps. 22:9-10)

To Jeremiah, God said:

> *"Before I formed you in the womb I*
> *knew you,*

> *And before you were born I*
> *consecrated you....."*   (Jer. 1:5)

To say that people come into this world alienated from God, denies Scriptural examples like these.

6. The doctrine of original sin is inconsistent with the Gospel. (Review chapter nine to see this clearly.)

7. Another reason for rejecting the doctrine of inherited spiritual death can be added at this point. You will notice that the following discussion corresponds very closely with the preceding argument; however now, instead of merely talking about forgiveness of sins, I am emphasizing the condition of spiritual life or death.

Consider the Christian understanding of the salvation experience. We believe that a person not only is forgiven of their sins when they receive Jesus Christ, but they also are "born again." Christians understand this to mean that they become *spiritually alive.* Indeed, Romans 8:10 tells us:

> *And if Christ is in you, though the*
> *body is dead because of sin, yet the*
> *spirit is alive because of righteous-*
> *ness.*

This belief that our spirits have been made

righteous and alive as we receive Jesus Christ is a fundamental truth of the Christian faith.

Consider then what would happen if two Christians—who are spiritually alive—have a baby. Are we to understand that the baby is born spiritually dead or spiritually alive? Well, the parents could not have passed on spiritual death if they both were spiritually alive. On the other hand, are we to believe that the baby born of non-Christians is spiritually dead? And what about the child born of a Christian and a non-Christian?

Please do not misunderstand what I am saying here. I am not saying that some babies are born spiritually dead, while others are born spiritually alive. No, what I am trying to show you is how illogical it is for people to say that every baby is born spiritually dead.

And yet that is exactly what Reformed Theology teaches. They teach that every baby comes into this world spiritually dead because of Adam's sin. What I hope you will see is how that belief contradicts a fundamental truth of the gospel, that Christians are made alive in Christ, and, therefore, are unable to pass on spiritual death to their children.

> You cannot be consistent and believe both the gospel and that all babies are born spiritually dead.

The only reasonable conclusion is that the condition of spiritual life or death is *not* passed like an inheritance between generations. What I will show you in the next chapter is how babies come into this world spiritually alive.

Each and any of the seven reasons listed in this chapter lead us to reject the doctrine of sin and death passed on inherently. However, we understand that sin and death have come into the world. We know that every human being sins. We believe that all people need Jesus as their Savior. We also understand that every human being is under the power of death, and, therefore, will die physically. However, we must reject the doctrine that says the sin and spiritual death of Adam are passed on inherently to all of humanity.

CHAPTER 12

Babies Are Alive

God told Adam and Eve that in the day they sinned they would die (Gen. 2:17). God did *not* say that all the generations after Adam and Eve would die spiritually. He said they—Adam and Eve—would die.

To apply God's warning to Adam and Eve as an automatic sentence upon all of mankind is wrong. We did *not* all die spiritually the instant Adam and Eve ate of the forbidden fruit.

What I want to show you now is that we die spiritually, not because of Adam's sin, but because of our own sin. We do not come into this world spiritually dead, but, rather, spiritually alive. We die spiritually when we, ourselves, sin.

Consider what God spoke through the prophet Ezekiel:

> *"The person who sins will die. The*
> *son will not bear the punishment for*

> *the father's iniquity, nor will the*
> *father bear the punishment for the*
> *son's iniquity; the righteousness of*
> *the righteous will be upon himself,*
> *and the wickedness of the wicked*
> *will be upon himself."*
>
> (Ezek. 18:20)

According to this verse, death is the result of one's own sin, not the sins of parents or ancestors who have gone before us.

Consider what the New Testament teaches us concerning this. Look again at Romans 5:12 and note how *death* comes to us:

> *Therefore, just as through one man*
> *sin entered into the world, and death*
> *through sin, and so death spread to*
> *all men, because all sinned....*

Death comes *through sin.* Of course, the first sin was Adam's. However, notice in this verse how death spreads to us. Paul said death spreads to all men, *because all sinned.*

Please note this carefully: People die spiritually, because of their own sin, not because of Adam's sin. Death came into the world because of Adam's sin, but it did not come into you and me until we sinned. That is when we died spiritually.

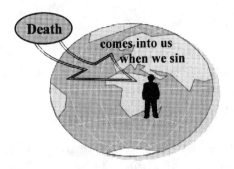

Death does not spread as a result of a person's birth, but rather as a result of his/her own sin.

God told Adam and Eve that in the day they sinned they would die. The same applies to us: "For the wages of sin is death..." (Rom. 5:23). When Paul wrote of these "wages," he was referring to the consequences *of our own sins.*

The apostle Paul made this clear from another perspective when he explained in chapter seven of Romans how sin becomes active in our being whenever we place ourselves under the Law. Rebellion then rises inside of us. Sin then leads to death.

> *And I was once alive apart from the Law; but when the commandment came, sin became alive, and I died.*
> (Rom. 7:9)

Did you hear that? Paul said that he was once *alive.* When did he die? The death of which he speaks did not come as a result of inheriting spiritual death from Adam. No, it came as a result of his own sin when he rebelled against the Law of God.

Spiritual death comes upon us as we sin.

What I am saying is that a child is born *spiritually alive*. However, when a person commits his or her own sin, that is when he or she dies spiritually.

Of course, every human being commits sin during his/her lifetime. Therefore, everyone needs the forgiveness of Jesus Christ. They also need the rejuvenating life of Jesus to restore them to life. They need to be born again.

What we are determining, however, is the very basic nature of man. I am saying that babies come into this world spiritually alive. When a child is conceived, the energy and the genetic information necessary to create a new person is passed from parents to child; however, a new soul is created innocent and alive.

Reformed Theology does not acknowledge this. The associated teachers wrongly teach that babies are born in sin, with an inherited nature to sin, corrupted to the core of their being, marked by original sin, alienated from God and spiritually dead. When Reformed teachers say that "we all died in Adam," they are implying that every human being died spiritually, and that we all deserve to be sentenced to hell eternally as a result of Adam's sin.

Christian leaders who teach this are put in a very awkward position when discussing babies who die before or shortly after birth. All of us want to believe that babies go to heaven when they die. However, if a leader is going to stay consistent with his belief that all people die in Adam, they have to follow through to the inescapable conclusion that babies go to hell if they die.

Augustine made room for water baptism as a means of escape, teaching that if a baby is water baptized, the sin and guilt of Adam will be washed away, and then the child will go to heaven if he/she dies.

Roman Catholics followed Augustine's teaching that water baptism can wash away the sin and guilt of Adam, but they also went a step further, teaching that babies who die without being water baptized go to "limbo," a place of happiness, but forever separated from the presence of God. Limbo is said to be a much better place than hell; however, the state of eternal separation from God is an unavoidable conclusion as long as they continue to believe that babies are stained with sin and alienated from God through the sin of Adam.

Reformed Theology rejected the idea that water baptism of infants could erase the sin of Adam from a child's heart. Being true to their belief that only a personal salvation experience could redeem an individual from the stain of Adam's sin, they held to the position that babies who die go into eternal damnation.

There is no other conclusion which can be drawn logically if, indeed, man is alienated from God and evil to the core because of Adam's sin.

A troubling reality is that a large percentage of Christian leaders are not consistent in their own beliefs. A certain minister may teach on Sunday morning that every human being is born in sin, but then before the week is over have to perform a funeral for an infant, at which time he may tell everyone that the child is in heaven. When a leader does this, he contradicts his own teaching.

Either babies are alienated from God and spiritually dead, and hence, go to hell; or else they begin spiritually alive and go into the presence of God when they die.*

I believe the second one.

As I have been attempting to explain throughout this book, the doctrine of inherited sin came from mistranslations and misinterpretations of the Bible. The truth is that babies come into this world spiritually alive. People die spiritually, not as a result of Adam's sin, but as a result of their own sin. This is what the Bible says: *"The person who sins will die...."* (Ezek. 18:20a). The obvious point is that *you cannot die unless you are first alive.*

> You cannot be consistent and believe both that babies are born spiritually dead and they go to heaven if they die.

---

* These issues become even more significant when we consider the millions of babies that are aborted each year.

CHAPTER 13

Who Is God?

The topics I have been discussing have far-reaching ramifications. Number one is our concept of God.

Think for a moment about a God who would send millions—even billions—of babies to a place of torment because of Adam's sin. Although Reformed theologians may prefer not to talk about this aspect of their theology, they cannot escape it. If they hold to a belief that "all die in Adam," then they have to say that all who leave this world without first receiving Jesus Christ will be eternally separated from God. In plain words, dead babies go to hell. Think about this— if you dare. The God whom Reformed theologians must sell to us is inconceivably cruel.

The fact that many of the forefathers of the Christian faith have taught this is so grievous to me now that I am weakened in my spirit just to write these words.

Let's make a comparison. If you were to accuse your neighbor of abusing his child, it would be a very serious accusation. It would be even more alarming if you announced it to the community or publicized it in the local paper. Whether or not it is true, the public notice of child abuse would tarnish the reputation of that neighbor.

Reformed Theology has declared and maintained before the whole world that God will hold all people accountable for the sin of Adam. For centuries they unashamedly have held to their conviction that as a result of Adam's sin babies who die will be cast into hell.

What does that say about God? What about His reputation? Is that really who God is?

Some may respond, "I don't want to think about this." Indeed, it would be easier to avoid talking about the implications of our doctrines. This is too unsettling. It would be easier to continue preaching what we always have preached without questioning the ramifications.

But how can we continue to be silent on such a grave issue? If the implications of our own doctrines are too troubling to face, then it is time we ask if there is something wrong with our doctrines. Indeed, if the implications of a doctrine are not true then that doctrine cannot be true.

Furthermore, the mission of the Church, first and foremost, is to declare who God is and to reconcile people to Him. Concerning His nature, we must represent Him accurately. Concerning reconciliation, we must ask, "Do people want to be friends with a God who torments babies forever?" These are no small issues. Please, brothers and sisters, do not run from this.

Consider the nature of God as revealed in the Bible. Examine Him. See if, indeed, He is the kind of God who would send millions of babies to hell.

I already discussed His great declaration from Mount Sinai concerning who He is. As God descended to meet with Moses, the mountain quaked and the earth trembled. Do not forget what He spoke. Above all else, know that He is the kind of God whose lovingkindness extends to thousands, while He would only allow sin to reach to three or four generations, and even then, only upon those who hate Him.

He is a good God.

Some may cower under this declaration from Mount Sinai and continue to shout back, "But He is also just!" In shouting this to us, they will imply that justice demands God punish the whole human race because of Adam's sin. They would hold their position in the face of God's own voice from heaven.

Look then more carefully at *justice*. Does it demand that all the human race suffer for the sin of Adam? No. Justice *by definition* means that punishment is correctly assigned to the offender. That is what justice is.

God has declared repeatedly in His Word that He will render to every man according to his deeds (*e.g.* Rom. 2:6; Ps. 62:12; Matt. 16:27). Listen to that, "according to his deeds." Babies have done no deeds. Will they be sent to hell for Adam's deeds? No! That is not justice!

Then let's turn our eyes from Mount Sinai and look to Calvary. There we have an even clearer revelation concerning who is God. The only begotten Son of God died on a cross for the forgiveness of our sins. This One, we are told, is the exact representation of the Father. Picture Him.

God loves mankind. He is not willing that any should perish.

The apostle Paul gives an argument in the book of Romans to which we would be wise to pay attention. He wrote:

> *He who did not spare His own Son,*
> *but delivered Him up for us all, how*
> *will He not also with Him freely give*
> *us all things?* (Rom. 8:32)

Paul is asking the reader to think about the goodness of God. If we catch the spirit of his exhortation, we can almost hear him say, "Use your head." Paul is pointing out that God was so good to us that He gave His own Son to die on the cross. Realizing this, Paul is asking us to consider the implications. In other words, he is saying, "Does it make any sense that He would not give us all things freely?" If He gave us His Son, certainly He would help us in all ways.

That is the kind of God we have. He has done everything possible, beyond forcing our wills, in order to bring mankind to Himself. God has gone to great extents to save us.

Yet, Reformed Theology says that God will send babies to hell without even giving them a chance. Does that make sense to you? Use your head! The doctrine of original sin and the inevitable consequences contradict the revelation of God, which we have in the Bible and in Jesus Christ.

God is love. This does not mean He merely is capable of loving. Rather it means His very being consists of and emanates love. Like the sun emits light, God emits love. It is His nature.

Is it, therefore, reasonable to think that God sends babies to hell? Is this love? Is this justice? No. Settle this issue in both your head and heart.

> You cannot believe all of these:
> God is love, God is just and He sends babies to hell.

Our understanding of man's nature has an impact not only upon our concept of God, but upon every area of theology and Christianity, including our concept of the world, salvation, evangelism, ourselves and how we are to live the daily victorious Christian life. I will discuss those areas in the last four chapters of this book. But first I need to continue developing an accurate biblical view of sin and man's nature. In this endeavor, I will attempt to keep our investigation in line with a revelation concerning the goodness and justice of God. All truth must come into alignment with the revelation concerning who He is.

CHAPTER 14

The Power of Sin and Death

I have been teaching that sin and death came into the world as a result of Adam's sin, rather than into the inherited nature of man. Let's go on to see the workings of this sin and death in the life of the individual.

After Adam and Eve disobeyed God, we can see how sin worked in the life of Cain. God warned Cain, saying:

> *"...sin is crouching at the door; and its desire is for you,...."* (Gen. 4:7)

Notice that God did *not* say, "Sin is inside of you now that your parents have sinned." No. God warned Cain that sin was *outside* of him waiting to come into his life.

It is also significant to note God's description that sin's "desire is for you." Sin is not an inert, passive or imaginary entity. It is *active*.

When I label sin as *active* I do not want to imply that man is helplessly subjected to its power. Cain had a choice to open himself to the sin or reject the sin which was crouching at his door. Sin is active but every human being has a free will.

In the New Testament, James explained the correlation between a person's own desires and sin:

> *But each one is tempted when he is carried away and enticed by his own lust. Then when lust has conceived, it gives birth to sin; and when sin is accomplished, it brings forth death.*
> (James 1:14-15)

Notice the process: desire grows into lust which leads to temptation which leads to sin.

A person's natural desires are not evil, but when an individual gets carried away by those desires it may lead to sin. In the example of Cain, he had emotions of anger toward his brother, but he did not sin until he gave into those passions to the end that he killed his brother. So, then, desires are not evil but they give opportunity for temptation. If a person yields to temptation, sin is given birth, or in other words, it comes alive.

Paul referred to this active nature of sin in the New Testament. He explained how "sin became alive" in his life (Rom. 7:9). Further, he wrote "for sin...deceived me, and through it killed me" (Rom. 7:11). Again, we see that sin is not passive, but actively working upon all of mankind.

Following sin comes death. Or we can say that sin is the *doorway* through which death may enter and work upon a person. Paul explains that "death spread to all men, because all sinned" (Rom. 8:12). James wrote the same truth saying, "...when sin is accomplished, it brings forth death" (James 1:15).

Sin and death work together corrupting mankind. Referring to their effect upon man, Paul talked about the "law of sin and death" (Rom. 8:2). In making this reference to "law," Paul is not talking about the type of law which man chooses to obey or disobey. Rather, he is referring to a law comparable to the law of gravity. As gravity causes things to fall downward, so also sin and death act as forces pushing people in negative ways.

A good analogy is like that of a dam standing against a wall of water. When a person comes into this world, he/she is like a dam having no holes. However, when cracks form in a dam, the water begins to flow, and that flow can grow stronger and stronger through the holes. In similar fashion, people may open themselves to sin and its influence by an act of their own free will. As they do, the power of sin may become stronger and stronger in their lives.

This power of sin and death is not just floating in the atmosphere. It is a real force, yet it also works through people. As I mentioned earlier, sin is at work through our parents, friends, teachers, leaders, entertainers, movie makers, etc. As they yield to the evil influences at work in this world, they also become avenues by which evil works on others around them. Sin and death are active throughout the world and in the people around us.

Sin and death exert a corruptive force upon every human being. We even can say, "Sin is corrosive." Paul explained how there was a law of sin at work in the members of his body (Rom. 7:23). As a consequence, his body became a body of death (Rom. 7:24). These forces are real and we all experience them in our daily lives. All humans will succumb to the power of death. All of us in various ways submit to sin during our lives.

Death entails more than physical death. It involves the corruption of a person's entire being. As a man yields to the power of sin, death even will reach into the spirit of man, to the end that he dies spiritually.

A good analogy is that of an apple which has been cut and exposed to the air; in a short time the apple's interior will turn brown. In similar fashion, people become corrupted as they open their hearts to the evils of this world.

That is where our *sin nature* originates. We are not born with it. God does not bring us into this world with the sin of Adam instilled within our nature. No! Our sin nature grows in us as we each yield to temptations, and hence, allow sin and death to work within us.

In other words, we choose the course of our own lives. Some people become very corrupt by submitting to sin repeatedly. Other people yield in less serious ways, but they also open themselves to sin and develop a sin nature.

As I discuss this process, do not let go of our underlying truth which is the main point of this book: *that people come into this world created in the image of God and that the nature of man is basically good.* Here I am simply explaining how each person becomes evil—it is as they yield to the power of sin which is in the world.

As we envision people choosing good or bad, I do not want to make it seem like an all-or-nothing process. No one chooses good every minute of every day: "for all have sinned..." (Rom. 3:23). On the other hand, people can choose evil but this does not necessarily make them "totally" corrupt. They still may have some good qualities (as I will discuss in chapter 22).

Furthermore, people can change during their lifetime. They may live righteously for a period and then yield to sin's influence for a time. Later they may repent and live lives more in keeping with God's will (Ez. 18:21-24). People have a free will; therefore, they can change.

Even the power of the sin nature within a person may change. As people yield to sin, they may give themselves over to such an extent that they no longer can control their own behavior. On the other hand, people can resist sin, and as a consequence, weaken the power of sin which is at work in the members of their own bodies. Furthermore, through Jesus Christ they can find forgiveness and cleansing for the sins which they have committed (I John 1:7-9). It is beyond the scope of this book to explain it fully, but this is included in what we call the process of sanctification.

Of course, we realize that no one can live perfectly. No matter how hard one tries, he/she still will fail. We all need forgiveness for the sins we have committed, and complete cleansing is only available through Jesus Christ.

CHAPTER 15

Man's Free Will

In spite of being wonderfully created by God, we all sin. Solomon stated it well:

> *"Behold, I have found only this, that God made men upright, but they have sought out many devices."*
> (Eccl. 7:29)

People make choices during their lives. At times they yield to the power of sin which is in the world. They choose evil.

Some would take this as proof that man *is evil*. They simply cannot comprehend how man would choose evil if he were not evil already. The error of their thinking is revealed if we just consider Adam and Eve. We know that they were created innocent and good, yet they chose to sin. One does not have to *be evil* to *choose evil*. No. All he has to have is a free will. The fact that we all sin is not proof that we are evil, but proof that we do, indeed, have a free will.

In the previous chapter, I used the analogy of a dam standing against a wall of water. When a person comes into this world, he/she is like a dam having no holes. However, when a crack forms in a dam, the water begins to flow and that flow can grow stronger, enlarging the holes, and making the flow even stronger.

Using this analogy, those who believe man is born evil would have to say that man is born already having holes in his dam. In fact, they would have to say that man is born already saturated with water, that is, saturated with sin. Yes, Christians who agree with Reformed Theology actually believe this.

Those who teach the total depravity of man will say that man's will is so inherently corrupt, that every decision is made with some underlying evil motive—*even our righteous acts are as a filthy rag.* Total depravity means totally and completely evil. Therefore, in the mind of the Christian who follows Reformed Theology, an unsaved person has no free will not to make every decision with a deep underlying selfish motive.

Do not miss the seriousness of this error. In the minds of Christians who believe in total depravity, the will of man is so inherently perverted and twisted that man is incapable of choosing good. Do you see how this negates free will? You cannot believe in total depravity and at the same time believe man has a free will.

Those who reject total depravity, but still think man is born with a *tendency to sin,* have a similar problem. They envision man making daily decisions but in every decision man will have a *tendency* to seek his own pleasure, and hence, go against God's will. Even this position is impossible to hold while at the same time believing in man's "free" will. If man is inherently "bent," then he is not inherently "free." You cannot believe both.

Make no mistake concerning the reality of man's free will. Man's ability to choose is a fundamental characteristic of being created in the image of God. We can choose. As recorded in the Old Testament, God said:

> *"...I have set before you life and death, the blessing and the curse. So choose life...."*   (Deut. 30:19)

If it were not possible for man to choose and do good, then God would not tell us in this verse, as well as hundreds or even thousands of other passages, to make such choices.

Man does have the ability to choose; therefore, he is not inherently bent toward evil nor depravity. I trust you realize the significance of the truth I am presenting here. Earlier I explained why a Christian cannot believe in the gospel and believe in original sin. I also explained why the gospel is inconsistent with a belief in inherited spiritual death. Here I am pointing out that a Christian cannot believe in man's free will, and at the same time, believe that man inherits a sin nature. The two are mutually exclusive beliefs. Therefore, we have to reject the doctrine which says man is born with a nature inherently bent toward evil.

> You cannot be consistent and believe both
> that man is born with a free will
> and man is born with a sin tendency.

However, a final point should be added here: man can *become bent* as a result of previous decisions. For example, a person may give themselves over to sin—so much so that sin becomes a lifestyle and, in fact, difficult to resist. On the other hand, people can make good choices continually during their life, to the extent that they become prone toward future good decisions. They choose their lifestyle.

In summary, we are saying that man is not inherently bent toward evil, but he becomes bent toward good or evil through the ongoing exercise of his free will.

God's Influence

The discussion in the preceding chapter about man's free will is neither complete nor accurate unless I also talk about the role of God in determining man's decisions. God is sovereign. He can and does intervene in the lives of people, guiding and even forcefully directing their daily lives.

Consider, for example, the life of Jeremiah. God spoke to him, saying:

*"Before I formed you in the womb I
    knew you,
And before you were born I
    consecrated you;
I have appointed you a prophet to
    the nations."*   (Jer. 1:5)

God chose Jeremiah before he even was born. God predetermined the role Jeremiah would fulfill in life.

85

Many a parent has sensed the hand of God upon their child. This may be the result of the parent's prayer, as in the life of the prophet Samuel (I Samuel 1:9-20), or it may be the sovereign choice of God to act in a person's life.

For another example of the dealings of God, look at the life of Jonah. Even though Jonah ran from the presence of God, God pursued him until he submitted. Only after going through great trials did Jonah finally obey God and go preach to the city of Nineveh. God did not allow Jonah to be completely free to determine his own actions.

For a New Testament example, we can look at Saul/Paul. He was persecuting Christians until Jesus powerfully appeared to him and turned his life in the opposite direction. In that appearance our Lord said to Saul, "It is hard for you to kick against the goads" (Acts 26:14c). To understand this, we should note that goads were sharp instruments used to prod oxen to go where their masters wanted them to go. This statement from our Lord implies that He had been prodding Saul down a specific path. Even though Saul was resisting the prodding of God, God continued working with him. However, at the appearance of our Lord to Saul, the prodding turned into an even greater, more powerful influence upon his life.

Whether we talk about God's choice from before birth, as in Jeremiah's life, or His ongoing dealings with men, as with Jonah and Saul/Paul, we can see that God does not allow people complete freedom to do whatever they want to do. He can and does intervene at times.

This, however, does not mean that God predetermines every person's actions and daily decisions. Certainly there are examples of people in the Bible whom God did influence and even sovereignly direct. However, we cannot take God's dealings with certain individuals and apply them to all people at all times. There is no basis for saying that God deals with *every* human being in such a directive manner. All we can conclude with certainty is that God *can* and *does* intervene when He wants to do so.

Indeed, Scriptures imply that God deals differently in different people's lives. He is a personal God. Philippians 2: 13 tells us:

> *...for it is God who is at work in you, both to will and to work for His good pleasure.*

From verses such as this one, we understand that God works in the heart of every Christian.

Indeed, many other Bible passages talk about God guiding, leading, drawing, speaking, encouraging, discipling and even forcefully directing the lives of His children.

I also can mention that God can influence and direct the lives of evil men and women. For example, Pharaoh, who lived in Moses's time period, is said to have been hardened in his heart by God so that God could use him to fulfill His purposes (Rom. 9:17-18). It is unclear from

Scripture how much Pharaoh hardened his own heart and how much God, by a sovereign act, hardened his heart, but it is undeniable that God was actively involved in turning Pharaoh's heart, that is, determining Pharaoh's will.

We also can read in the book of Romans, about evil men and women who continually gave themselves to sexual sins, until "...God gave them over to a depraved mind..." (Rom. 1:28). Obviously, these people were choosing evil by an act of their own will, but we also can recognize the role of God where He actually stepped in and not only let them go toward depravity, but *turned them* over to it.

Other passages talk about God blinding the eyes of certain people (*e.g.*, Rom. 11:8-10). In these incidents the will of the individuals is involved to different degrees, but we cannot deny that God does intervene, both stirring and, at times, forcefully determining the lives of people.

The main point I am making in this chapter is that man is not entirely "free." God can intervene if and when He chooses. Proverb 21:1 tells us that even the heart of the king is in the hand of the Lord. Yes, God can "bend" the will of a person.

However, notice from whence the bending of man's will comes. I am not saying that man's will is bent because of Adam's sin. The bending comes from heaven, not the Garden of Eden. We may be bent by God, but not by Adam.

CHAPTER 17

Weak And Flawed

To this point we have established certain truths about mankind's nature. We are created in God's image and maintain some degree of glory. People have a witness of God instilled within their nature, knowledge of the truth of God and natural desires to do God's will. We are neither born in sin nor with original sin. Babies come into this world innocent, uniquely associated with God's presence and spiritually alive.

We also have noted God's description of Adam and Eve, that they were "very good." However, we discovered that they still were vulnerable to sin (Gen. 1:31). In similar fashion, we come into this world good, yet vulnerable in our natural condition.

Remember the analogy which I used of a dam standing against the pressure of the water? We come into this world like a dam—no holes, but weak and soon to form cracks. Furthermore, like the water behind the dam, sin has power. It is corrosive. We, who are weak, are unable to resist.

In addition to this general vulnerability of all people to sin, we also must acknowledge that individual people do inherit specific weaknesses and frailties. Just as some people are born with susceptibilities to certain diseases, so some people seem to be born with a susceptibility to alcoholism, anger, depression, overeating, sexual perversions or other negative influences. They still have a free will, and, therefore, can submit to or reject these influences; however, some people seem to be weaker than others in certain areas.

These inherited weaknesses may go beyond just weaknesses and actually be tendencies within a person to choose evil in some specific area or areas of his/her life. Hence, we can call these *character flaws*. This is where we would recognize that the sins of parents can be passed on to the third and fourth generations.

I am not saying that man inherits a sin nature from Adam. That is not so. God said He would *not* allow sins to be passed on to many generations. I am simply acknowledging that specific sin areas in a parent's life may release their influence upon descendants three to four generations later. Please recognize the distinction I am making between inheriting a sin nature and inheriting specific flaws in one's character. Reformed Theology teaches that man inherits evil *throughout his entire being* which influences every single decision, in every area, every day. I have rejected that way of thinking. However, I am (and I hope you are) embracing a view of man which acknowledges certain negative tendencies in specific areas of a person's life which may have been established by parents, grandparents and/or great-grandparents.

Understand that character flaws are one step deeper than character weaknesses. A weakness implies an inability to resist some evil which is outside of a person. A character flaw, on the other hand, implies a negative quality actually resident within a person's being.

Let's summarize what I have said by contrasting the views of man's nature which I have presented. Those who hold to total depravity believe that man's every decision has an underlying evil motive. Those who teach that man is bent toward sin believe man will have a tendency to choose evil with every decision. I am presenting a view of man as being basically good by God-instilled nature, but also weak and/or flawed in different areas.

Of course, I also should mention the position which is at the opposite extreme of total depravity. That would be total goodness. As Bible-believing Christians, we cannot accept that view, because everyone sins during his/her lifetime, and all fall short of the glory of God (Rom. 3:23).

Biblical View
of the Natural Man

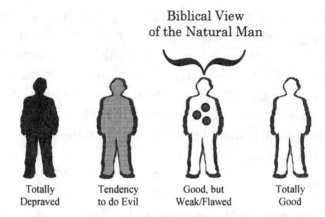

| Totally | Tendency | Good, but | Totally |
| Depraved | to do Evil | Weak/Flawed | Good |

I hope you can embrace the view which sees man as starting out in life basically good, while at the same time having weaknesses and character flaws. This view sees man as susceptible to the evils which are resident in the world; it also makes room for the negative influences which can be passed on for three or four generations. This is what the Bible presents to us as truth.

Finally, we should not think of inherited weaknesses and/or flaws as entirely negative, for it is these which most obviously reveal our need for a Savior. Therefore, in some ways weaker people have an advantage over those of stronger character because they more readily may see their own need to look to God for the salvation of their own souls.

CHAPTER **18**

The Nature of Jesus

Christians influenced by Reformed Theology like to make a strong contrast between the nature of Jesus and the nature of the rest of mankind. They point out that Jesus was born of God and that all the rest of mankind has descended from Adam. As a consequence, they will say that Jesus had no sin nature, but every other human being has a nature totally corrupted by sin. This contrast is so important to Reformed Christians that they sometimes present it as a fundamental truth of their faith.

We know that Jesus was conceived as the Holy Spirit came upon the virgin Mary (Luke 1:26-35). Jesus is the only begotten Son of God (John 3:16). In contrast, all the rest of humanity is descended from Adam.

However, it is biblically incorrect to see the nature of Jesus and the nature of man as completely different from each other. We are told in the Bible that "the Word became flesh" (John

1:14). Paul taught concerning our Lord, saying:

> *...although He existed in the form of*
> *God...emptied Himself...being made*
> *in the likeness of men.* (Phil. 2:6-7)

Jesus took on human nature.

In what way did Jesus have our nature?

According to Reformed teachers, Jesus was born with a perfectly holy nature, while the rest of mankind is born with a perfectly corrupted nature.

Yet the Bible tells us that Jesus Christ was tempted like every other person is tempted:

> *For we do not have a high priest who*
> *cannot sympathize with our weak-*
> *nesses, but One who was tempted in*
> *all things as we are, yet without sin.*
> (Heb. 4:15)

Jesus experienced temptation. He felt the pull of temptation.

If Jesus had no sin nature how could He have been tempted like all other people? If man is prone to sin like the Reformed teachers say, but Jesus was not prone to sin, how could He have been tempted in the same way we are?

Do you hear the contradiction at this point in Reformed Theology? If man has a sin nature and Jesus did not, He never could have been tempted in all ways as we are. Therefore, He could not be our high priest able to sympathize with our weaknesses as Hebrews 4:15 reassures us.

Do not misunderstand what I am saying here. I am not implying that Jesus had a sin nature. On the contrary, I am showing you another reason why we cannot accept a doctrine which says that mankind inherits a sin nature from Adam.

> You cannot be consistent and believe that man is born with a sin nature, Jesus is born without a sin nature and Jesus was tempted in all ways as we are.

Reformed teachers wrongly think that a contrast between the nature of Jesus and the nature of the rest of humanity is necessary. Of course, we know that Jesus was born through the supernatural encounter of the Holy Spirit with the virgin Mary. All the rest of mankind has descended from Adam. However, there is no reason that we must see man's condition at the opposite extreme from our Lord's. To contrast our Lord's condition with man's does not make Jesus any holier or purer. He is holy because He is the only begotten Son of God.

CHAPTER 19

A Closer Look

I have been teaching that man does not *inherit* a sin nature from Adam, but rather he *develops* a sin nature by yielding to sin as an act of his own free will. In other words, man starts out right with God, but turns away from Him as he grows and makes choices to sin.

Reformed Theology teaches something very different. Christians under this way of thinking see mankind as totally corrupt and that this evilness is inherited from Adam. Every baby comes into this world selfish, and, therefore, antagonistic toward God.

Who is right?

There are certain Bible verses which we need to examine more carefully because they are typically used by Reformed thinkers to teach their doctrine that all men are corrupt from birth. Let's discuss those verses and show how they teach something very different than total depravity.

For example, Reformed teachers like to quote Romans 3:10-12, which says:

As it is written,
"There is none righteous, not even one;
There is none who understands,
There is none who seeks for God;
All have turned aside, together they
have become useless;
There is none who does good,
There is not even one."

Those who believe that man is totally depraved use these verses to emphasize the evilness of man.

Of course, we believe that every human being sins. However, notice how we are told in these verses that all have "turned aside." They have "become useless." You can't turn aside unless you are first turned in the proper direction.

This is in keeping with Paul's teaching in chapters one and two of Romans. Remember what we discovered when we studied these chapters earlier? Paul explained that people begin in life with:

1. a witness of God
2. knowledge of the truth of God
3. natural desires to do God's will

Having established these truths, Paul went on in chapter three of Romans to explain that we all *turn away* from the natural, God-instilled orientation.

The reason many Christians misinterpret Romans 3:10-12 and wrongly think that man comes into this world totally evil is because they jump to chapter three instead of first studying the truths Paul laid out in chapters one and two. When we study those chapters first, we see that man is oriented toward God in his natural state. Later he turns away from God.

Recall what we are told in Ecclesiastes:

> *"Behold, I have found only this, that*
> *God made men upright, but they*
> *have sought out many devices."*
> (Eccl. 7:29)

This verse gives us the same perspective that Paul does in the book of Romans. People start out right, but then turn away from God.

Another verse often used—or rather misused—by Reformed thinkers is Romans 3:23:

> *...for all have sinned and fall short*
> *of the glory of God....*

Those who believe that man is evil like to quote this verse, but in stating this, they apply it as a sentence on man's nature—as a declaration that man is sinful by creation.

That is not what Romans 3:23 says. In fact, it tells us that we fall short *because we sin*. We do not fall short because of *Adam's sin*. No. It is *our own sin* which disqualifies us.

Again, we cannot separate Romans 3:23 from chapters one and two where Paul taught that people start off in life with a nature oriented toward God. Our problem is that we *turn away*. We *fall* from glory.

Another verse in Romans often misinterpreted is 7:18:

> *For I know that nothing good dwells*
> *in me, that is, in my flesh....*

Some Christians take these words of Paul and from them mistakenly teach that nothing good dwells in any of us.

To see that this is the wrong interpretation, all we have to do is read the context of Paul's words here. Throughout chapter seven, Paul is explaining the conflict that happens within him because both good and evil are at war. Several times in that chapter, Paul mentions the *desire to do good* or the *wishing to do good* that is within him (*e.g.*, Rom. 7:15, 21, 22). Seeing how many times he refers to this good element within his own being, we have to conclude that his words, "nothing good dwells in me, that is in my flesh," do not refer to his *entire* being. There is also a good part.

Flesh refers to the carnal, corrupted, evil part of our nature. Therefore, by definition, there is nothing good in our flesh. However, it would be wrong to say that our entire being is fleshly. That would contradict what Paul was saying about the conflict of good and evil within him. There is no conflict if there is no good. Both good and bad exist within a person. Flesh is the bad portion.

If you previously have interpreted Romans 3:10-12, 23, and 7:18 through the eyes of those who believe in totally depravity, please reconsider. Read the context. Start in chapters one and two where Paul explains the God-oriented nature of man. Don't confuse man's condition after sinning with his inherited nature. Yes, we are sinners; but no, we did not inherit this condition.

One last Bible passage which is sometimes misinterpreted by those who teach total depravity is Ephesians 2:1-3:

> *And you were dead in your trespasses and sins, in which you formerly walked according to the course of this world, according to the prince of the power of the air, of the spirit that is now working in the sons of disobedience. Among them we too all formerly lived in the lusts of our flesh, indulging the desires of the flesh and of the mind, and were by nature children of wrath, even as the rest.*

The phrase, "by nature children of wrath," is sometimes used to teach that all people are inherently evil. A careful examination will show us just the opposite.

Notice in these verses where sin finds its source: it is in the world, coming from the prince of the power of the air. Evil comes as a result of the evil spirit being allowed to work in people. As people yield to the evil in the world, by living according to their lusts, then they take on a nature of wrath.

Of course, people can have a nature of wrath; however, they are *not born* with it. No. They become evil (wrathful) when they yield to or choose evil. Yes, we do have a sinful nature, but it grows within us as we yield to sin which is in the world.

Furthermore, our sin nature is not *all* of our being. There is also a good part—the original part—that which has been instilled within us by God. We were created in God's image; however, we have become, to some extent, corrupted—not evil through and through, but "tainted."

This will become even more clear in the remaining chapters.

CHAPTER 20

What Is Sin?

Our understanding of man's nature is very much determined by our definition of sin. The Greek word used in the New Testament from which our noun "sin" is translated is, *hamartia* (*harmartano* when a verb). Literally, this Greek word means *missing the mark*. When this phrase, *missing the mark,* is used today, two very different images form in the minds of Christians. Those who have been influenced strongly by the Reformed Theology of the 1500s think something very different than those who share the view I am presenting in this book.

Those with a Reformed view envision God's will as something similar to a bullseye on a target which is difficult and seldom hit. Because they believe in total depravity, the Reformed thinker sees non-Christians as never hitting the bullseye and always sinning with every action and decision throughout their day. Christians are envisioned as being closer to the target's center, but only occasionally hitting the exact bullseye of God's will. Sin is seen as something which we do constantly, with only an occasional departure into God's perfect will. In fact, Reformed teachers often say, "Man sins every minute of every day, in thought, word and deed."

In contrast, those who share the view of this book see sin very differently. They do not see God's will as a small bullseye on a target in front of them. Rather, God's will is much broader in scope. For example, a mother taking care of her child is, in some measure, doing God's will. Similarly, the father working to provide for his family probably is doing what God wants him to do. There are, however, temptations along life's path. Each person makes choices whether or not to veer off of course and, hence, sin. Those sins may be in thought, word and/or deed; however, they are seen as departures from the normal established flow of life.

These differing views of sin (*missing the mark*) influence a person's understanding of many Bible verses and biblical concepts.

For example, Romans 5:8 tells us:

> *But God demonstrates His own love toward us, in that while we were yet sinners, Christ died for us.*

Our question concerning this verse focuses on the word, *sinner*. In the mind of the Christian who believes man is totally depraved, all people are sinners because all people sin all the time, continually. In the mind of those with a more positive view of man's nature, a sinner is someone who sins once in a while or even often— however, not *constantly* with every thought, word and deed.

Compare our use of the word *sinner* with how we use a word such as *teacher*. Is a teacher someone who teaches all day long, never taking a break? Or is a teacher someone who teaches once in a while? Obviously, we can use the word either way. The word teacher does not tell us the frequency in which the activity of teaching actually is engaged. In similar fashion the word "sinner" can be used for a person who sins constantly or occasionally.

Those who believe in total depravity see in the word "sinner" (as used in verses like Romans 5:8) someone who sins continuously and constantly. Christians who believe man is basically good see a sinner as someone who sins once in a while. Realize that both groups of Christians see all people as sinners. The difference in their views has to do with their different definitions of the word "sinner."

Not only is the word "sinner" interpreted differently, but our understanding of other specific Bible passages also changes depending upon our view of man's nature.

For example, Romans 14:23 says:

... whatever is not from faith is sin.

In the mind of the Christian influenced by Reformed Theology, this verse says that everything anyone does, unless it is motivated by, and/or undergirded with faith, is sin. This view places all or the vast majority of man's activities and thoughts under condemnation.

If we read the context of Romans 14:23, we see a different—more accurate—meaning. Throughout the fourteenth chapter of Romans, the apostle Paul was talking about behaviors which some Christians consider evil and others consider acceptable. For example, some Christians were restricting their diet while others ate anything. Paul was not trying to condemn any specific behavior in this chapter, but rather exhort Christians to be sensitive to one another and not do something which would cause their brothers and sisters to stumble. It was in that context that he said, "...whatever is not from faith is sin."

What we see by reading the context of Romans 14:23 is *not* that faith must be behind each and every thought or action of a person. Rather, Paul was instructing the early Christians how to deal with situations in which some Christians thought a specific behavior was wrong and others thought it was okay. He was giving them a guideline on which to base their decisions on such matters.

This more accurate interpretation of verse 23 is clarified by reading what Paul said in the verse just preceding it:

*The faith which you have, have as
your own conviction before God.
Happy is he who does not condemn
himself in what he approves.*

(Romans 14:22)

Notice when we should be happy—when we eat
and drink things and don't feel guilty about it, or
when we are living our lives without guilt
tormenting us about what we do.

According to Romans 14, what is sin? Is it
any action or thought which is not backed by
faith? Or is sin knowing that something is wrong
and then doing it anyway? I believe the latter is
what Paul is teaching us in Romans 14. The
Reformers were taking this verse out of context
and misinterpreting it. They were wrong.

Those who believe in total depravity tend to
see God as a God of perfection who demands
perfection from His subjects. When they define
sin as missing the mark, they are envisioning a
God who has placed before mankind a tightrope
upon which he must place one foot in front of the
other, never missing the mark, that is, never
missing the next step on the rope. Every step off
centerline is sin in the Reformer's eyes—and,
hence, in the eyes of the God whom they present.

In contrast, those who hold to the view of sin
I am presenting see God allowing people much
freedom to act and grow up in life. They please
God simply by living and enjoying life. However,
there are tests, trials and temptations along the

way. People sin when they respond to those tests contrary to the will of God. Rather than walking a tightrope, people are walking through life, which in a very natural way pleases God; however, there are tests along the way which people fail or pass; that is, they sin or don't sin.

Those who believe man is totally depraved envision the non-Christian doing every single thing during the day contrary to God's will. They view the Christian as a person who has gone through a change of heart and, therefore, wants to please God; however, he is unable to do so very often.

In contrast, the Christian with the positive view of man's nature, which I have been presenting, sees man (the Christian and non-Christian) as doing many good things throughout his life but occasionally sinning. Some people sin more than others. The Christian has forgiveness for the sins he has confessed to God, and the work of the Holy Spirit in his life is leading him down a road to greater and greater sanctification. The Christian life is one of doing much good, but occasionally missing the mark.

Finally, we can see this proper view of sin by reading the biblical promise of forgiveness:

> *If we confess our sins, He is faithful and righteous to forgive us our sins and to cleanse us from all unrighteousness.* (I John 1:9)

This is a wonderful promise. There is great hope here.

However, this promise cannot be true if man is as evil as the Reformers say. If people sin every moment of every day in thought, word and deed, no one ever could confess every sin. If what the Reformers believe about man's nature is true, no one could be cleansed of *all unrighteousness* at any one given moment.

The Reformers are wrong. The Reformers' definition of sin and their understanding of man's nature does not fit the Bible. Man is not as bad as they imagine.

CHAPTER 21

Look at Life

We have been examining Scriptures from a new perspective and learning how man is basically good. Now let's consider some real life experiences and see how these biblical truths actually reveal themselves.

For example, picture George who starts his day by getting out of bed, taking a shower, getting dressed, and then sitting down for breakfast. There are hundreds of decisions he must make just to arrive that far in his daily routine. Are those decisions evil or good?

Taking a shower for example: Is this a totally depraved decision, one bent toward evil, or basically good in God's eyes?

In the mind of the Christian trained under Reformed Theology, George is taking a shower for the underlying motive of selfishness, perhaps to feel good or to impress people so he can further his own evil goals throughout the day.

Those who believe man's will is bent toward sin also will see in George's decision to shower an underlying motive bent toward self, and, therefore, sin.

In contrast, the Christian with a positive view of man's nature will see George taking his shower as something which probably is according to God's will. In fact, George's natural desires to clean up, get dressed and eat breakfast are basically God-instilled, good desires.

The Christians with a positive view of man's nature will admit that on some days George may have corrupted or perverted motives, even in his morning routine. For example, George may put on a little extra cologne one morning in hopes of catching the heart of some unsuspecting woman at his place of work. George even may make several decisions during his morning routine which are influenced by more evil goals. However, such negative decisions are seen as departures from the normal, basic, instinctive and even decided actions of his day.

Take one more example—say of a mother caring for her newborn. Is she totally depraved, bent toward evil, or one who is bent toward good, but doing evil from time to time? When she rises to help her child, is that action pleasing or displeasing to God?

In the mind of the Christian who believes in total depravity, "all of our righteous deeds are like a filthy garment" (Is. 64:6); therefore, even such actions (which appear to be good) are evil in God's eyes.

Those who believe man is bent toward sin also would suspect the mother of having evil motives right at the heart of her behavior—whether it is to selfishly raise a child for her own purposes, or to be seen by others as a good mother, or to have the personal satisfaction of thinking she is a good person—all of these are considered evil.

In contrast, those with a positive view of man's nature believe that the God-instilled desires of a mother to care for her child are good, and, therefore, it pleases God when a mother yields to those natural desires. Of course, a certain mother may choose to stray from the natural paths, and, consequently, harm her child or simply do some action in selfishness, but those would be departures from the natural good within her nature.

The truth is that the vast majority of mothers are good to their children and want the best for them. Selfish actions, such as abandoning children or abusing them, are infrequent, and, in fact, are reported in the news when they are discovered because they are such alarming departures from the norm.

In discussing real life situations such as these, we are addressing the question, "How evil are people?" Are they evil to the core of their being? Are they evil every minute of every day in thought, word and deed, as the Reformed teachers would have us believe? No. On this issue, Reformed Theology is wrong.

CHAPTER 22

Evil People

Our perspective acknowledges that people start off good, but are weak and/or flawed. They become bad or evil as they harden their hearts, deny the witness of God, and turn away from doing good. Some people become very bad. Let's consider some examples.

The Bible describes a person who has been wounded in his/her heart and how he/she may become corrupted. We all have seen examples of this, such as the person who has been abused as a child, and, hence, developed serious emotional, psychological and moral problems. Similarly, an adult may go through a tragic divorce, and later act very wickedly toward his/her ex-partner. Also, we can read the warning given to us by the writer of Hebrews as he tells Christians not to allow a root of bitterness to arise within their hearts (Heb. 12:15). Indeed, when any such heart defilements enter a person, they may bring about evil thought and behavior patterns.

Of course, there are some individuals who simply choose a lifestyle which is contrary to the will of God. These may be in line with character flaws or weaknesses in their own nature. They may result from the negative influences of other people surrounding their lives. Or they simply may be lifestyles chosen without any previous indications.

I also can mention that some people show evil behavior when they become emotionally, physically and/or spiritually exhausted. For example, the mother who has spent all her energy caring for her little ones may lose her temper and hurt her own children. A business-man on the verge of losing everything may turn against those around him and strike out violently. A man in war may be so overcome by his surroundings that he becomes almost animal-like in his survival tactics and actions toward others.

Christians who believe in total depravity would point to these last examples of people acting at the limits of their strength and offer the following explanation. They would say, "You don't know what is in a man until he is so exhausted that the evil is revealed." Those who believe in total depravity would point to that person acting out of animal instincts as the true man—exposed and evil to the core.

I disagree with that explanation. Man is more than that. Yes, he does have instinctive survival and self-preservation tendencies at the core of his nature, but he is also the one who cares for his family when sane. A mother is the one who loves her children and would do anything for their welfare and success. Exhaustion does not reveal the true person, but rather leaves a person without the strength to act like they really want to act, or to be who they really are.

Similarly, we can talk about people with psychological disorders. There are compulsive liars, schizophrenics and even psychotic killers out there. We would label many of them as very evil. Some even may have given themselves over to demonic influences.

However, even most of those with serious psychological disorders should not be labeled as "totally depraved." Many of them do not want to do the evil which they find themselves doing. Furthermore, many can be helped by treatment with certain medications. If they were totally depraved, no amount of physical treatment would help in any way. If they were totally depraved, then the evilness would be in every fiber of their being—inherited and inescapable.

When speaking of evil people, I prefer to use the words "tainted" or "corrupted" rather than "totally depraved." Yes, there are some very evil people in the world. However, even most of them will have some positive characteristics.

For example, consider those locked away in our prisons. When we watch television portrayals of what goes on inside prisons, we often see the most wicked side. Personally, I do not believe those dramatizations are very true to reality. In my experience dealing with prisoners and ex-convicts, I have seen that the majority have many positive characteristics. If you build a relationship with someone in prison, you will discover that many of his/her concerns are related to the welfare of his/her family. Most of them are not entertaining evil thoughts 24 hours each day. No. They probably committed a crime to be confined in that place, but the majority have friends, thoughts about God and desires to do better with their lives in the future.

It is easy to form a negative view of people when we frame our perception by what is presented through a few television programs. Even the news media—which endeavors to present facts—only shows a narrow view of life. For example, we may hear of the terrorist who bombed some airplane and killed many innocent people, but for every terrorist there are thousands of other people riding airplanes in peace, not wanting to hurt anyone. In fact, the majority will be giving a smiling face to the person seated next to them, and they will be happy to help an elderly person lift their bag into the storage bin. That majority rarely makes the news.

Of course, there are a few really evil individuals out there—but very few. The truth is that most people cannot even think of someone they know personally that they actually could label as a *totally* evil human being. Can you? If so, write their name on the following line:

_____

Most people have no name to write. They have heard of someone in the news who has committed some evil deed, or they may have watched a television program that portrays a psychotic killer. However, most people cannot name even a single person whom they personally know that they would clearly label as a totally evil human being.

Considering the possibility that you might know one, or maybe two, individuals whom you would label as totally evil human beings, contrast this with how many other people you know.

Of course, we all sin and fail during our lifetimes. We need forgiveness for the sins we have committed and we need the power of the Holy Spirit to conquer future temptations. However, the truth is that sooner or later most Christians come to the realization that even their non-Christian friends have good qualities.

Indeed, there are a few people whom we would consider very evil. However, when we use the term "evil," I hope you will see it as "tainted," rather than totally corrupt.

CHAPTER 23

Good People

In the beginning of this book, I pointed out that Jesus spoke of both evil and good people. For example, our Lord said:

"...He causes His sun to rise on the evil and the good, and sends rain on the righteous and the unrighteous."
(Matt. 5:45)

If we are going to see people as Jesus sees them, we must acknowledge that both evil and good people are in the world.

In recognizing good people, we are admitting that there are good people without reference to a redemption experience. As Christians, we understand that forgiveness of our sins and a transformation of our hearts come through the redemption made available through Jesus Christ. However, we also need to acknowledge some degree of goodness in people, apart from the redemption experience.

For evidence of this, I can point to numerous examples in the Old Testament of people who are recognized as good, even though they had not yet learned of Jesus Christ. For example, the first verse in the Book of Job tells us:

> *There was a man in the land of Uz, whose name was Job, and that man was blameless, upright, fearing God, and turning away from evil.*
>
> (Job 1:1)

Consider what the Bible says about Noah:

> *Noah was a righteous man, blameless in his time; Noah walked with God.* (Gen. 6:9b)

Concerning Josiah, who became the king in Judah, the Scriptures say:

> *And he did right in the sight of the LORD, and walked in the ways of his father David and did not turn aside to the right or to the left.*
>
> (II Chron. 34:2)

Similarly, King Amaziah "continued to seek God" (II Chron. 26:5). King Jotham "did right in the sight of the LORD" (II Chron. 27:2). Enoch "walked with God" (Gen. 5:22). And while Jehoshaphat was king, people from all the cities of Judah gathered together "to seek help from the LORD" (II Chron. 20:4). Of course, we also could study King David, who had a heart after God, who often inquired of the Lord and who sought Him with all his heart.

The above-mentioned people did not receive their goodness as a result of a salvation experience. No, they had not yet heard about Jesus Christ.

There are many other examples I could mention here, but my point has been made—there are many good people mentioned in the Old Testament. In fact, when the prophet Elijah cried out to God in despair, thinking he was all alone in serving God, our Lord answered him, saying, "I have kept for Myself seven thousand men who have not bowed the knee to Baal" (Rom. 11:4). These are God's words. God told Elijah that around him—in his time period and in his region—there were 7,000 people faithful to the true God.

When I talk about people being good (apart from the redemption of Jesus Christ), I am not saying they are perfect. No, every human being sins. All need forgiveness, which is only available through the death and resurrection of Jesus Christ. However, we still should acknowledge the fact that there are good people.

It is worth pointing out that even the *heart* of man can be good. Our Lord Jesus talked about the positive aspect of people's hearts:

> *"Blessed are the gentle...the merciful...the pure in heart...the peacemakers...."*   (Matt. 5:5-9)

> *"...these are the ones who have heard the word in an honest and good heart...."*   (Luke 8:15)

Yes, Jesus believed some people have an honest, good and/or pure heart.

Some Christians today have only negative thoughts concerning the heart of man. Reinforcing their negative view, many have fixed their mind on a verse from the book of Jeremiah which says:

> *"The heart is deceitful above all things, and desperately wicked: who can know it?"*   (Jer. 17:9 KJV)

Indeed, this verse talks about how evil the heart of man can be.

However, to take this one verse and apply it to *all* people as a description of *all* men's hearts is wrong. To see how wrong that is, all we have to do is read the context of Jeremiah, chapter 17, and see that the preceding two verses talk about righteous people:

> *"Blessed is the man who trusts in the LORD
> And whose trust is the LORD.*

> *For he will be like a tree planted by*
> *the water...."* (Jer. 17:7-8)

Of course, the heart of man *can* be deceptive, but it also can trust in God.

Consider this. When Jeremiah said the heart of man is "deceitful," do not interpret this word to mean "totally evil." Instead, think how easily a person can deceive him/herself. For example, a person who is committing a sin easily can rationalize that sin in his own mind. As the Bible says, "All the ways of a man are clean in his own sight..." (Prov. 16:2). The heart of man is deceitful in the sense that any one of us can justify our own actions to ourselves.

That is the message of Jeremiah 17:9. In the very next verse God says:

> *"I, the LORD, search the heart,*
> *I test the mind,*
> *Even to give to each man according*
> *to his ways, according to the*
> *results of his deeds."*
> (Jer. 17:10)

Do you see what is being addressed here? Man can deceive himself, but God can see the truth. By saying man's heart is deceitful and wicked, Jeremiah was not saying that every human being is totally evil. No. He was pointing out how easily we can fool ourselves, but we can't fool God.

The tragic point for our discussion here is how some Christians today would claim for all people—including themselves—a totally evil heart. They misinterpret Jeremiah 17:9 and remain fixated there. Therefore, they despise and mistrust their own heart, when in reality they may be one of the blessed ones who trust in God, described by Jeremiah in the previous verse.

Finally, consider our Lord's words in Matthew 7:17-18:

> *"Even so, every good tree bears good fruit; but the bad tree bears bad fruit. A good tree cannot produce bad fruit, nor can a bad tree produce good fruit."*

Jesus was not talking about just trees here. He was speaking figuratively of people. The truth is that many people do produce good fruit. Therefore, they are good.

Indeed, there are many good people.

CHAPTER 24

People Are Loveable

Take a broad look at society. For example, imagine yourself standing on a hill overlooking a city. What do you see? Some will see masses of people struggling for survival, selfishly hurrying about to make money, and only caring for themselves—creatures of habit, instinct and evil desires.

That is not an accurate view, nor is it the way God wants us to view humanity. Stand on the same hillside and look out at the masses of people. Now, see precious people: parents who go to work every day and try to provide for their families; teachers in schools trying to educate the children; mothers watching over their little ones; thousands driving the highways, most of whom are moving in an orderly fashion, trying to obey the laws and not hurt others. There are people working in hospitals and nursing homes, carpenters and businessmen, police officers and storeclerks. Most people are spending their days working and doing their best to live and succeed. In the evenings, the majority of individuals are not out stealing or committing murder or adultery. There are some, but most are at home with their families or just enjoying some type of relaxation. The vast majority of people are fairly decent, law-abiding citizens.

This is reality.

I have traveled in many nations around the world, and everywhere I go, I see good people. In every community I find people willing to help and give. Whether we are in a huge metropolitan area or a remote village in the jungle, people are working and laughing and trying to get along with others. Parents everywhere want their children to succeed. Husbands and wives want to get along and have a good marriage. People want to live in peace with one another. The vast majority of people on the earth want to do good, and they are trying. They fail from time to time. They are weak and they give into various temptations. But they are basically good. That is how God created them.

As a matter of fact, I dare say that *people, for the most part, are creative, productive, funny, friendly, helpful, kind, wonderful and precious.*

This last statement is in stark contrast to the view of man put forth by Reformed Theology. Consider, for example, the description of man promoted by Martin Luther. While explaining the salvation experience, Luther would use an analogy saying that man is similar to a pile of cow manure, but when a person is saved it is as if they are covered with a layer of snow so that the ugliness no longer can be seen.

Of course, we can admire the clear, powerful teachings Martin Luther offered concerning salvation by grace through faith. However, his concept of the nature of man is wrong. Man in his natural state is not like cow manure.

May I suggest a better, more accurate analogy? Picture many automobiles lined up at a mechanic's shop, all needing to be repaired. Some cars cannot be moved because they have flat tires. Others have broken radiators or fan belts. Others have dents due to collisions, and others just need a tune-up to run better. Of course, some of those automobiles have more serious problems, and they will require major work done if they will ever run again. People can be compared with those automobiles. They all have problems. They all need repairs.

However, this analogy is more accurate than Martin Luther's because people are not cow manure. They are valuable. They are worth fixing. If we equate man with manure, it implies that there is nothing of value in man. Of course, Luther's comparison makes God's love for us seem even greater and more undeserved, which may be a wonderful way to view His love.

However, is man valueless? Does God save cow manure? No!

Man does not *deserve* God's love; however, man is *worth* loving. Please note this distinction.

The automobiles in our analogy do not *deserve* to be fixed, for they can do nothing to earn the privilege, right or blessing of being repaired. However, those automobiles are still valuable. Most of them are probably *worth* fixing.

People are much more valuable than automobiles. No one *deserves* to be forgiven of their sins or saved from judgment. However, God thinks that we are *worth* saving. Both good and bad people are worth saving. In fact, He thought enough of us to send His only begotten Son to die for us. We were created in His image and He decided that image is worth redeeming.

Yes, your neighbor is valuable. People are precious. You are worth loving. *There is something of value inside of you that God likes.* It is not just that God loves what is unlovable, which is, of course, a true statement about His love. It is also true that *you are loveable.*

CHAPTER 25

Your Worldview

Some Christian readers may hesitate to accept the positive view of man's nature which I have been presenting because they know that certain non-Christian groups teach the inherent goodness of man. For example, humanistic philosophy and modern New Age thinking espouse this doctrine. Christians today realize that these are contrary to Christianity in many ways, and, therefore, they may reject what I am saying because it sounds like something humanists or New Age advocates would teach.

Please note that I am not taking my thoughts from humanism, New Age ideas, nor other cultish philosophy. I am developing my understanding from the Bible. That is the foundation upon which I am standing.

Why is the positive view of man so important? I already have discussed how it influences our concept of God (chapter 13). In the next chapter we will see how it fashions our relationships with other people. In chapter 27 I will discuss how our view of man determines our evangelistic methods. Then in the last chapter we will see how it influences our daily lives, putting us into bondage or bringing us into freedom. In this chapter I will explain how our view of man's nature determines our view of the world around us.

First, let's consider the non-Christian religions around the world.

If you think man is evil at the very core of his being, then you will reason that any attempt to reach God, which comes from man's own nature, is evil and, in fact, diametrically opposed to God. As the teachers of Reformed Theology, you would say that all of man's righteous deeds, including all other religions, are as a filthy rag in God's eyes. With that perspective, you will conclude that any religion, other than Christianity, is merely humanity's organized attempt to resist the true God.

On the other hand, if you think people are basically good, then you would expect that there is within man a natural tendency to seek God. In addition, you would expect to see a moral code, which is instinctively in man, being reflected in the beliefs which people develop. In that case, you would see some value to many of the other religions in the world. Of course, you still can recognize that the other religions are misguided and that the leaders have developed misconceptions concerning the nature of God; however, if you think man is basically good, you will recognize that there are some positive values in religions other than Christianity.

Please do not misunderstand what I am implying here. I believe in the positive view of man; however, I am *not* saying that "all religions lead to God." Of course, that is *not* what I am teaching. Jesus Christ is the Messiah, and there is no other name under heaven upon which we might call in order to be saved (Acts 4:12). However, as Bible-believing Christians, it is time that we ask, "What should be our evaluation of other religions?"

Obviously, there are certain religions, such as witchcraft, polytheism and idol worship, which are opposed to the God who is revealed in the Bible and in Jesus Christ. There are several religions mentioned in the Bible, such as the worship of Baal, which clearly are condemned.

However, consider Judaism. We know that the Jewish people as a whole rejected Jesus Christ as the Messiah. Therefore, they are not brothers and sisters in Christ with us. However, we also must remember that their religion was established by God in the Old Testament. It is not a system antagonistic toward God. Of course, they often rebelled against God, and they added numerous man-made traditions to their faith; however, the basic form of religion to which they cling did not grow out of man's evil nature. It was God's plan given to them through Abraham, Moses and other religious leaders. The Ten

133

Commandments were written in stone by God Himself. Jewish people traditionally have held to high moral values which are very much in line with God's will. Furthermore, the Bible indicates to us that thousands of people who followed the Jewish religion in Old Testament times were in some fashion pleasing to God (*e.g.* II Chron. 20:13-22; Rom. 11:4).

As we study cultures other than Judaism we learn that many of them developed a system of moral codes. In fact, many ancient civilizations had codes which sound very much like the Ten Commandments. This is understandable to us when we realize that God placed some consciousness of right and wrong in each of us.

Consider the Islamic religion which today claims one fifth of the world's population. Are we to view their religion as evil or good? Of course we realize that they do not accept Jesus Christ as the Son of God, and, therefore, we understand that they are blinded to this most important truth. However, are they better off than the heathen who worships his ancestors or the one who does not even believe in God? Yes! There is some positive value in fearing and worshipping God, even if He is not understood accurately.

When we study the origin of the Islamic peoples, in particular the Muslims, we learn that their forefather was the son of Abraham through a servant named Hagar (Gen. 16). This son of Abraham was given the name *Ishmael* by God. Ishmael is a name meaning *Great*. We are told in

Genesis 16:11, that this favorable name was given to the forefathers of the Muslims because God was showing His favor to Hagar, who had been afflicted.

The compassion and heart of God towards the Muslim people can be seen in many other passages such as Isaiah 19:24, which says:

> *"Blessed is Egypt My people, and Assyria the work of My hands, and Israel My inheritance."*

Egypt and Assyria are countries at the very foundation of the Islamic religion. Yet notice how God claimed them as His own people right along with His claim to Israel.

Next, consider God's dealings with the city of Nineveh. During the Old Testament times this city was perhaps populated by several different groups; however, being a major city in Assyria, a large percentage of the people were most likely descendants of Ishmael.

God sent Jonah to preach in Nineveh. In response, people repented and turned to God. Afterwards God relented from His anger and showed His compassion to the people (Jonah 3-4). This tells us much about God's attitude toward these people who were neither Jew nor Christian.

Even more enlightening is how God spoke with Jonah after the people of Nineveh repented. Jonah was disappointed that God did not destroy the whole city. God then spoke to him, saying:

*"And should I not have compassion
on Nineveh, the great city in which
their are more than 120,000 persons
who do not know the difference
between their right and left hand, as
well as many animals?"*

(Jonah 4:11)

God loved the people of Nineveh. In contrast,
Jonah thought the heathen people should be
destroyed.

Of course, Jonah was wrong. The question we
should ask ourselves is, "What would our
attitude have been toward the people of
Nineveh?" Or more importantly, "What do we
think about people who pray to God even though
they are not Christians?"

Consider Cornelius (neither Jew nor
Christian, but a Gentile) about whom we read in
Acts 10. We are told that he was devout and
God-fearing. When an angel appeared to him, the
angel reassured him that his prayers had been
heard by God (Acts 10:4). This is eye-opening
because it indicates that God does, at times, hear
the prayers of non-Christians.

After having an encounter with Cornelius,
the apostle Peter had a major change in his
whole concept of non-Jewish people. Previously
he thought, as other Jews did, that only they
were accepted by God. Consider Peter's words:

"I most certainly understand now that God is not one to show partiality, but in every nation the man who fears Him and does what is right is welcome to Him."
(Act 10:34b)

Peter had a major revelation! He completely changed his concept of people who believed differently than he. He realized that they, too, were welcome to God.

Many Christians today need a similar revelation. There is value in fearing God. God does, at times, answer the prayers of non-Christians. In fact, all God-fearing people, no matter where they live on this earth, are "welcome to Him." (I am not saying that they are "saved"—I just am repeating what the Bible tells us, that they are "welcome.")

These examples should open our eyes to see how God views the non-Christian and non-Jewish world. He responds to them and shows them compassion.

In contrast, Christians influenced by Reformed Theology tend to see the whole (non-Christian) world as antagonistic toward and totally alienated from God. They see the natural man as unable to do anything positive or pleasing to God. They see all of man's attempts to please God as "filthy rags."

The obvious point is that the worldview of Reformed Theology does not match God's

137

worldview. In other words, Reformed Theology is wrong on this issue.

Having a negative, rather than a positive, view of man's nature has implications not only for one's concept of the whole of humanity and the religions of the world, but it also leads to negative judgments on specific areas of society. If a Reformed thinker follows his own beliefs through to the logical conclusions, he must reason that whatever the natural man develops from out of his own efforts ultimately will be evil.

This includes government. Christians who hold to the basic evilness of man tend to see every governmental system as corrupt or, at best, a "necessary evil" in the earth.

In contrast, the New Testament teaches us that government is a "minister of God" (Rom. 13:4). Of course, we know that corrupt individuals may be involved and even hold positions of authority; however, the apostle Paul teaches us that every government that exists has been established by God (Rom. 13:1). The proper biblical view is that we should see government as the hand of God reaching into the earth to establish peace and order.

Similarly, how we view the business world is determined by our concept of the nature of man. If we believe man is evil to the core, then we will see the whole business world as a mass of greedy individuals striving for self-satisfaction and self-glorification. On the other hand, those who believe man is basically good at the core of his being, will see much good in the midst of the world's business activities and affairs.

To make a point on these issues, I would like to ask you to consider who establishes the will of God on the earth more effectively today—the Christian Church, other religions, government or business? Of course, we believe that the Christian Church carries the message of salvation through Jesus Christ and this message can, from the eternal perspective, accomplish far more for humanity than anything else. However, let's consider other aspects of God's will. Around the world who is more responsible for establishing His will? Let's take specific areas which we know God desires for mankind.

For example, we know God does not want people killing each other. Who then is more responsible for stopping murder in the earth? The Church? Non-Christian religions? Government? Or Business? The answer is government. The various governments across the earth do more than any other entity in keeping people from killing each other.

The next question has to do with people cheating and stealing from one another other? Who is most active and successful in establishing this aspect of God's will? Of course, the Christian Church teaches moral ethics. However, remember that only about a third of the world's population is under the direct influence of Christianity. Most other religions also teach moral standards. However, the truth is that the various governments also play a major role in hindering people from cheating and stealing.

How about establishing God's will on the earth in the areas of providing people with homes, clean water, sanitation and clothing? The Christian Church helps in these areas; however, government and business do far more in providing these blessings from God on the earth.

Who is more responsible for providing education to the five to six billion people on this earth? Primarily government.

Who is more responsible for giving people ways to earn money so they can provide for their families? Government and business.

Who is more responsible for providing people with security in their homes, cities and countries? Government.

Who is more responsible for providing for and ensuring that elderly people are taken care of? In most countries it is either the family or government.

Who is more responsible for providing fuel for your furnace, food in the local grocery store, medicine and medical treatments? Government and business.

I could go on, but I have said enough to make my point. A realistic view of the world reveals to us much good coming out of government, business and even non-Christian religions. These things are not completely evil.

Reformed thinkers tend to view as evil everything which develops from out of man's nature. In addition to the the areas I have mentioned, I could include art, music, scientific endeavors, efforts to bring world peace, attempts to preserve the environment, programs to feed the poor, progress, technology, etc. Once a person has embraced a negative view of man's nature, he/she will tend to think negatively about all of these things.

In reality, the world is not as bad as Reformed teachers would have us believe.

CHAPTER 26

Your Relationships

People's view of man's nature not only establishes their worldview, but it also fashions their relationships with others.

For example, people convinced that man is basically evil will tend to live in isolation. When they walk through the local shopping mall they will rarely, if ever, engage in conversation with strangers (unless it is for the purpose of converting them to Christianity). When they do business with a non-Christian, they will tend to suspect that person of trying to cheat them in some way. When they sit down with another individual and look them in the face, they have underlying suspicions that he/she may betray them. People convinced of the basic evilness of man never will be able to fully trust friends, family, co-workers or neighbors.

Reformed teachers sometimes justify their suspicions of others by quoting John 2:24-25, which says:

> But Jesus, on His part, was not
> entrusting Himself to them, for He
> knew all men, and because He did
> not need anyone to bear witness
> concerning man for He Himself
> knew what was in man.

Christians convinced that man is evil like to use
these verses, and then putting themselves in the
position of Jesus Christ, refuse to trust any other
human being.

That is a tragic misuse of Scripture. In the
context of these verses we see that the people
Jesus would not entrust Himself to were the
masses who were following Him because of the
signs they saw Him performing. Of course, Jesus
never could have entrusted His life to them. His
great mission to the earth could not even have
been put into the hands of His own disciples, for
even Peter gave our Lord bad counsel at one
point (Matt. 16:22-23). However, to equate our
personal situation to that of Jesus Christ's and
then posture ourselves above all the human
beings around us is a serious mistake.

We know that man is frail and subject to the
temptations of this world. However, living in
suspicion of everyone else is a terrible way to
live. People need people. That is how God created
us. In fact, our own frailties make it essential for
us to depend upon others. Proverbs tells us that
the wise man listens to the counsel of others (e.g.
Prov. 12:15). The apostle John explained how

having fellowship is like walking in the light, and it helps us become cleansed of sin (I John 1:7; 2:10). Open relationships are an essential part of a healthy life.

Furthermore, healthy relationships can only be developed if we have some assurance that people are *not* evil to the core of their being.

Think of your neighbors. How do you approach them? If you think your neighbors are evil, they will sense your suspicion and avoid you. They will judge you for judging them so harshly. It is very difficult to love what you think is evil by nature; therefore, you cannot reach them as easily with the love of God.

In the context of the local church, one's concept of man's nature strongly influences the depth of relationships. If leaders expect the congregational members to be basically evil, they likely will overemphasize submission to authority, and they may become very controlling. If the members think of their leaders or each other as evil, they will tend to keep themselves isolated and distant.

In such an environment, mistrust of others is justifiable and even reasonable. A dark cloud hangs over the church because the people must keep all of mankind in contempt. Usually it is subtle, and those involved are not even aware of how all-pervasive this way of thinking is in their own life. It is inescapable—Reformed Theology leads to an oppressive form of Christianity.

Recognizing the good in people's nature is essential.

Note the ramifications within the context of the family unit. For example, if a Christian woman believes her non-Christian husband is totally corrupt, what hope is there for them to ever have a good marriage? None.

If parents hold to a belief that their children are evil by nature, they will spend their energy trying to control or drive the evil out of them. On the other hand, if parents see good in their offspring and the possibility to walk up-rightly, their efforts will first be aimed at protecting the innocence of their young ones, and secondarily, at helping their children choose good. Indeed, our view of man's nature profoundly determines how we raise children.

It is also important to point out that people tend to become what they are expected to become. If we think people are evil we release pressures upon them to act and behave in negative ways.

For example, various people groups expect their children to act in specific ways. One group I have observed expect their teenagers to rebel and and then return to the beliefs and more civil behavior of their parents in their early twenties. Another group living in the same area expect their children to remain devoted and faithful to the beliefs of their family throughout their teenage years. It is amazing to see how the youth respond to and live up to these expectations put upon them by their elders.

Most of us have seen this principle at work within our own family units. Of course, family expectations do not completely determine the actions of an individual member of that family; however, it is undeniable that expectations are a powerful force.

This pressure can even be seen on the broader scale when we consider how many church-going people have very negative views of the non-Christian world. This is no small issue to the average guy sitting in the local bar drunk every night. Typically he knows full well that he is not doing what he should be doing. But in addition to his own guilt, there is tremendous pressure upon him, knowing that a large percentage of the people who do go to church consider him a failure, weak and disobedient to God. He lives under that pressure. It is real. He feels it. It beats him down and makes it even more difficult for him to overcome his problems.

The truth is that people tend to rise to the expectations placed upon them. If Christians expect non-Christians to be more evil than they actually are, they may actually be increasing the evil in the world. As we judge non-Christians, they tend to judge us. Of course, we know that everyone sins and fails during their lifetime; however, it is time we re-evaluate our view of people around us.

To put all this in perspective, consider the change which came in the thinking of Roman Catholics during the 1960s. Preceding that time,

Roman Catholics tended to look down on anyone who was not of their faith. Pope John XXIII did much to change that. One of his most profound statements was this:

> "The habit of thinking ill of everything and everyone is tiresome to ourselves and to all around us." *

In quoting this message from Pope John XXIII, I hope to draw attention to the change that happened in Catholics' minds—a change that took place after more than a thousand years of thinking very negatively about outsiders.

A similar change needs to happen in the minds of Christians influenced by Reformed Theology—their way of thinking is also *tiresome to themselves and everyone around them.*

---

* *Christian History,* Vol. XIX,, *John XXIII* by Elesha Coffman, page 31, © 2000, Christianity Today, Inc., Carol Stream, IL.

CHAPTER 27

Your Method of Evangelism

Some Christians may hesitate to accept the positive view of man which we are presenting because it seems to threaten their evangelistic methodology. By this, I am referring to the method many Christians have established for leading non-Christians to Jesus. Their method depends upon first convincing each person that he/she is dreadfully evil. They actually may think that a belief in the inherent evilness of man is necessary for continued effectiveness in evangelizing non-Christians.

Such thinking is in error. For evidence of this, consider the fact that Charles Finney, one of the best known evangelists in history, was a strong proponent of the view which says babies are born spiritually alive without inheriting the sin of Adam. The truth is that the basic goodness of man does not lessen the necessity for salvation. In fact, since man is born innocent, he is *more responsible* for his actions—his sins have been his own choice, not the fault of Adam.

An even better model and example than Charles Finney would be our Lord Jesus Christ. When He talked to people we do not see Him trying to convince them of their own sinfulness. In fact, as we read about Him talking to individuals one-on-one, we are surprised to see how easily He overlooked, forgave and almost minimized the sin issue (except for the sin of pride of which the Pharisees were guilty). Our Lord's de-emphasis on sin goes very contrary to evangelistic methods commonly used today which center on man's need for a Savior because of sin.

This vast difference between our current evangelistic methods and those of Jesus Christ is no small issue.

Our present evangelistic methods have grown out of our understanding of man's nature. Reformed Theology for years has taught that man is hopelessly evil and Jesus is the solution to that problem.

Of course, we all sin. Of course, we all fall short of the glory of God. But the first point of the gospel is *not* that we are sinners. No! Consider what is necessary for a person to be saved. The apostle Paul wrote:

> *...that if you confess with your mouth Jesus as Lord, and believe in your heart that God raised Him from the dead, you shall be saved.*
>
> (Rom. 10:9)

The key to salvation is not sorrow for sins committed, but rather a revelation that Jesus Christ is Lord.

It is irrelevant whether a person is good or bad; it does not matter whether they have sinned much or little—there is still only one way to the Father—through Jesus Christ. He is the Door. Good people or bad people—all need Jesus.

Think again of Cornelius who was said to be a righteous and God-fearing man. He, too, needed a Savior. Peter preached to Cornelius, saying:

> *"You know of Jesus of Nazareth, how God anointed Him with the Holy Spirit and with power, and how He went about doing good,.... And they also put Him to death.... God raised Him up on the third day....this is the One who has been appointed by God as Judge.... through His name everyone who believes in Him receives forgiveness of sins."* (Acts 10:38-43)

Notice where the emphasis is placed in Peter's presentation of the gospel. He explained who Jesus is. Sin was not the focal point of Peter's message. Of course, Peter ended by saying that everyone who believes in Jesus Christ will have their sins forgiven. But that is the *result* of believing in Jesus, not the starting point of his message.

151

Too often Christians reverse the order of their message. Since Reformed Theology has placed so much emphasis on the sinfulness of man, Christians today tend to start preaching from that point. A realization of personal sin need not be the starting point in a person's encounter with God. Whether or not they realize their own sinfulness, Jesus Christ is still Lord. When a person confesses with his/her mouth Jesus as Lord and believes in his/her heart that God raised Him from the dead, he/she will be saved.

The starting point of the gospel is not that man is a sinner, but rather that Jesus is Lord. If a person brings his/her life into submission to His lordship, they belong to Him.

The wrong emphasis in presenting the gospel has weakened our message. Of course, we want people to know that Jesus forgives sin. However, the more important message is that He is Lord. If a person comes to Jesus to worship Him as Lord, then their sins will be forgiven. In addition, their lives will come into submission to His lordship. If, however, they merely come to Him to have their sins forgiven, it is possible that they may never realize fully the significance of who He is. That is a mistake.

CHAPTER 28

How Then Shall We Live?

In this last chapter we want to discuss how one's view of man's nature determines his/her self-image, ability to make decisions, sense of peace and success in daily living.

If you think mankind is basically evil, you will have to hold yourself in contempt repeatedly and continually. When some other Christian quotes Jeremiah 17:9 and boldly declares that the heart of man is desperately wicked, you instantly will place yourself in the group of those whose hearts are evil.

How foolish and erratic! How much better to say, as King David said, "My heart trusts in Him" (Ps. 28:7).

How people see their own heart determines how they live their daily lives.

People who think their own heart is evil consciously or subconsciously mistrust themselves. They have little confidence in their own ability to make decisions. When they have stepped out with some positive action, they can be undermined at any moment by haunting questions, such as, "What if I am deceiving myself?" "What if this is just my own selfish desire?" Such Christians live with a *gnawing doubt* everyday of their lives.

Furthermore, they live with a constant internal war. Sincere Christians who are convinced of their own evilness must live their lives denying themselves and trying to conquer every desire which arises from within. Internally they are "at war." Though the Bible promises us peace, they never truly experience it in their own lives.

If they hold to the basic evilness of man, they must generate an entire system of thought around this concept. It becomes a form of Christianity which emphasizes control of oneself and others. Concepts such as dying to self and crucifying one's own desires become the repeated trumpet blast. Of course, there is some truth to the related teachings; however, under Reformed thinking these are usually *the focal point*. Non-Christians and Christians are repeatedly made to feel bad about themselves, and, hence, to "repent" again and again at the altar or simply in their own hearts. Since their foundation is a belief that man is inescapably evil, the continual and repeated conquering of one's own self is the only solution.

In contrast, Christians who believe their own heart is good will endeavor to bring to life and release that which flows within them. If they believe their natural desires are good, then they will trust and act upon those desires. They will consciously and subconsciously bring their daily decisions and actions in line with the desires, dreams and visions which they hold in their heart.

This second, more positive and confident lifestyle is liberating, fulfilling, powerful and fruitful. It is right!

In recommending this positive lifestyle, I am not giving credence to evil desires which have taken hold of a person through the effects of this world, past sins nor weaknesses passed on through family lines. We must continue to discern good desires from evil ones. I explained in chapter 14 the process of sin: desire grows into lust which leads to temptation which leads to sin. Realizing this, we must continue to hold our lusts in check. Furthermore, we know that the heart of man *can* be evil, and anyone—even Christians—can have evil thoughts and motivations.

However, in recommending the positive lifestyle, I am hoping to change people's focus. The *primary focus* of Christianity should be on releasing the good rather than conquering the bad.

In other words, go for your dream, follow your desires and trust your heart; however, keep alert for those tests along the way. Be watchful, but not paranoid. As King Solomon, the wisest man (other than Jesus) in the Bible, wrote:

155

And follow the impulses of your heart and the desires of your eyes. Yet know that God will bring you to judgment for all these things.

(Eccl. 11:9b)

This is how God wants us to live. This is how every good father wants his child to live—not under constant condemnation, but free, full of faith, energetic, yet watchful for deceptions and pitfalls along the way.

Can we really live this way? Can we trust that there is goodness inside of us? Consider the apostle Paul's words to the Romans:

And concerning you, my brethren, I myself also am convinced that you yourselves are full of goodness....

(Rom. 15:14)

Yes, this is what the Bible says. Yet, many Christians have no place in their theology in which to fit this truth. Their theology says it is not possible to be "full of goodness." Their theology is wrong.

I dare say to my brothers and sisters in Christ, the same words that Paul wrote: "I am convinced that you yourselves are full of goodness." Yes, you are good.

Conclusion

When a Christian programmed to Reformed Theology looks at a newborn infant, he/she sees a totally depraved child who inherited that evilness from Adam. In contrast, a Christian who embraces the view presented in this book sees a newborn infant as innocent, good and spiritually alive.

It is absolutely amazing how a person can look in the face of a newborn infant and see an image so strongly influenced by his/her theological training.

Just as amazing—or alarming—is how one's theological training can determine his/her view of the Bible. Two Christians can read the same Scripture and interpret it in very different ways, as we have seen in this book. I have shown you that the more accurate interpretation reveals to us the positive, rather than the negative, view of man.

I am not alone in holding this positive view. In addition to leaders such as Charles Finney, there have been various groups throughout Church history which have proclaimed that man is not inherently evil. Most known are those centered around the Pelagian controversy during the time of Augustine and the Enlightenment Period following the Protestant Reformation. In modern times a large percentage of the liberal teachers and theologians also believe in the inherent goodness of man.

Personally, I am not a liberal theologian, and I strongly disagree with many of the liberal positions. In particular, I hold firmly to the infallibility of Scripture. As Evangelical Christians, I believe the Bible must be our final standard for truth on such issues as this.

Unfortunately, most of my Evangelical brothers and sisters in Christ have interpreted the Bible verses relevant to these issues differently than I. Since the time of Augustine, the mainstream of Christianity has taught that man is inherently evil as a result of Adam's sin.

Realizing this, I know that I have been "walking on sacred ground." Some would even say that I have been *tromping* on sacred ground. I respect what the historical Church has believed and taught. Yet on this issue, I can not agree. For most of my own life I, too, taught that man is inherently evil. Changing over the last few years has been no small issue in my personal life. I have done much research, along with personal heart-searching. The implications of these issues are too significant to take lightly.

It is not that I now want people to look at humanity through rose-colored glasses. Rather I believe the Church has been looking through glasses which have distorted Her view. That distortion began in the time of Augustine and became so entrenched as a tradition taught in the historic Church that few even have dared question the related doctrines. By God's grace, I hope I can jolt others to reconsider the nature of man, and perhaps even help remove those darkened glasses now seated upon the Church.

Much of the argument concerning the nature of man centers around how we interpret the writings of the apostle Paul, especially the book of Romans. As I explained, the doctrine of inherited evil was developed in Augustine's time around a mistranslation of Romans 5:12. Also, those who follow Reformed Theology fixate on Paul's words in Romans 3:10-18 which expound upon the waywardness of man.

I have tried to refocus your attention, noting that Paul began his discussion in Romans 1 and 2 talking about how man originally comes into this world with some knowledge of God and natural desires to do His will. My perspective is that man *turns away* and *falls* short of the glory of God. Man is not born evil, but he becomes evil as he yields to the power of sin. Further, I have pointed out Paul's reassuring words toward the end of his letter to the Romans, where he declares that he is convinced the Christians reading his words are *full of goodness* (Rom. 15:14). In studying the beginning and ending of the book of Romans, we can see Paul's negative comments concerning man are sandwiched between very positive ones.

This leaves us with not only a positive view of how babies come into this world, but it also gives the Christian a hope of attainable goodness through the forgiveness of Jesus Christ and the ongoing work of sanctification.

This understanding of the book of Romans is not the only grounds upon which I stand. In chapters 9 and 11, I explained how a sincere Christian cannot believe the gospel and at the same time believe in the doctrine of original sin. This is shocking to many Christians, but it is inescapable. The two beliefs are mutually exclusive. I choose to believe the gospel.

Furthermore, I discussed the alarming implications of the doctrine of inherited sin; in particular, the inevitable conclusion that babies which die before or shortly after birth go to hell. This is unacceptable to most of us, and it leaves us with an image of a very cruel God—an image which contradicts the God who we see revealed in Jesus Christ.

The Reformed theologian's view of God even contradicts the revelation of God which we see coming from Mount Sinai. God told us that His lovingkindness would reach to thousands, but sin He only would visit upon three or four generations. In contrast, Reformed Theology teaches that the sin of Adam reaches to thousands of generations.

Any one of these arguments, or the others presented in this book, should be enough to change the minds of most Christians; however, to completely resolve the issues about man's basic nature, we must be relentless in our pursuit of truth. These issues are too significant. We are standing in the face of the historic Church which for the most part has held to the inherent evilness of man. We cannot simply push that aside and renounce it without being convinced fully, completely, without any doubt.

Knowing the frailty of man, I have done much soul-searching and, of course, I have considered the possibility that I have been viewing the Scriptures through my own limitations and biases. Because so many other Bible teachers—many who are more scholarly than I—have interpreted some of the same Scriptures in different ways, I have evaluated my own position again and again.

If it were just my own interpretation of various Bible verses on which I had to stand, I would continue, even today, to doubt myself in the face of so many others who have studied, researched and come to different conclusions.

However, there is more to it than that. In the first chapter of this book, I pointed out our Lord Jesus' perspective concerning the people who lived in His time. He referred to good and bad people. There is no interpretation necessary to understand that. Our Lord recognized good people. Every argument on the inherent evilness of man crumbles in light of His words. Even if my own interpretations of various other Bible verses are distorted by my own frailties, I cannot deny the words of the One whom I call "Lord."

Furthermore, Jesus stated that the angels of children are constantly beholding the face of the Father. Because of His teaching, we cannot hold to a doctrine which says babies come into this world alienated from God.

His words have nailed closed the coffin door on the doctrine of the inherent evilness of man.

Now another door is open—a door which reveals mankind and all of the world in a more positive light. The implications are profound and far-reaching. So now, walk through the door and let this truth set you free.

DEVELOPING A PROSPEROUS SOUL

VOL I: HOW TO OVERCOME A POVERTY MIND-SET

VOL II: HOW TO MOVE INTO GOD'S
FINANCIAL BLESSINGS

There are fundamental changes you can make in the way you think which will release God's blessings. This is a balanced look at the promises of God with practical steps you can take to move into financial freedom. It is time for Christians to recapture the financial arena.

SPIRITUAL REALITIES

Here they are—the series explaining how the spiritual world and the natural world relate. In this series Harold R. Eberle deals with issues such as:

- What exists in the spiritual world
- Discerning things in the spirit
- Interpretation of dreams
- Angelic and demonic visitations
- Activities of witches, psychics and New Agers
- Spiritual impartations and influences between people
- Understanding supernatural phenomena from a biblical perspective
- Science and the Bible: Creation, forces, time, discoveries in quantum mechanics,...

- How people access that realm
- Out-of-body experiences
- What the dead are experiencing
- Christian perspective of holistic medicine

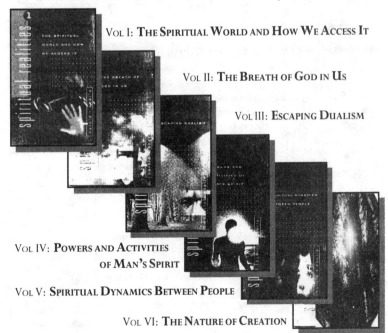

VOL I: THE SPIRITUAL WORLD AND HOW WE ACCESS IT

VOL II: THE BREATH OF GOD IN US

VOL III: ESCAPING DUALISM

VOL IV: POWERS AND ACTIVITIES
OF MAN'S SPIRIT

VOL V: SPIRITUAL DYNAMICS BETWEEN PEOPLE

VOL VI: THE NATURE OF CREATION

PRECIOUS IN HIS SIGHT *A Fresh Look at the Nature of Man*
During the Fourth Century Augustine taught about the nature of man using as his key Scripture a verse in the book of Romans which had been mistranslated. Since that time the Church has embraced a false concept of man which has negatively influenced every area of Christianity. It is time for Christians to come out of darkness! This book, considered by many to be Harold Eberle's greatest work, has implications upon our understanding of sin, salvation, Who God is, evangelism, the world around us and how we can live the daily, victorious lifestyle.

YOU SHALL RECEIVE POWER

Moving Beyond Pentecostal & Charismatic Theology
God's Spirit will fill you in measures beyond what you are experiencing presently. This is not just about Pentecostal or Charismatic blessings. There is something greater. It is for all Christians, and it will build a bridge between those Christians who speak in tongues and those who do not. It is time for the whole Church to take a fresh look at the work of the Holy Spirit in our individual lives. This book will help you. It will challenge you, broaden your perspective, set you rejoicing, fill you with hope, and leave you longing for more of God.

DEAR PASTORS AND TRAVELING MINISTERS,

Here is a manual to help pastors and traveling ministers relate and minister together effectively. Topics are addressed such as ethical concerns, finances, authority, scheduling,.... In addition to dealing with real-life situations, an appendix is included with very practical worksheets to offer traveling ministers and local pastors a means to communicate with each other. Pastors and traveling ministers can make their lives and work much easier by using this simple, yet enlightening, manual.